The Unknown Knowns

Ian Hall

Orchard House
Books

Published by Orchard House Books 2015

Orchard House Books
Raven Lane
Applethwaite
Keswick
CA124PN

The right of Ian Hall to be identified as the author of this work
has been asserted by him in accordance with the Copyright, Design
and Patents Act 1988

For Jennifer, in rueful recognition of the hardships involved in living with someone who won't stop questioning his religion.

CONTENTS

Acknowledgements

For an initial introduction to the I Ching, back in the 1990s, my thanks to the late W. S. Boardman who lived in Ravenglass on the Cumbrian coast, who was a friend and the author of what is in my opinion still the handiest booklet for simply consulting the I Ching – 'The Pocket I Ching', published by Penguin under their Arkana imprint: ISBN 0-14-019049-X. In it Stan Boardman distils the Wilhelm/Baynes translations of the sixty four readings onto a double page for each.

For their helpful comments on the ordering of chapters and better definition of themes, thanks to James Ramsden, Phillip Sturgess and Howard Bowron; and for meticulously proof-reading, improving the sense of the argument, and general encouragement, my thanks to Robin Taylor. Thanks to Robin also for additional references. Any mistakes remaining are mine alone.

For continuous encouragement, putting up with my absent-mindedness when deep in thought, and sharing her own insights into the theme of our collective unconscious my thanks, as ever, to my wife Jennifer.

Thanks to her too for the cover photograph.

The Unknown Knowns

Overview

God and Religion: what emotions do those words raise in you?

Apathy? – They are irrational and irrelevant to my life.

Indignation? – Why do people get so worked up about religion?

Warmth? – God is the mainspring of my life, and my religion is hugely important to me.

Aggression? – How can other people not see that my religion's image of God is the only true picture?

Anger? – Most of the wars ever fought have been over religion. How can people be so cruel in defence of a loving God?

Perplexity? – How can a loving God allow such suffering?

And so on... the reality is God and Religion can stir every emotion known for each of us at various times in our lives. This book is based on the premise that this is because God, whether or not He/She/It exists as an external reality and 'first great cause', most certainly exists as an internal reality, deep in our unconscious brains.

Defending this premise, and working on from it, will lead us into several different disciplines, requiring at least an amateur introduction to ancient religions, Jungian psychology, the Chinese Book of Changes (the I Ching), DNA, and quantum mechanics. We will see how Carl Jung, the eminent Swiss psychologist of the first half of the Twentieth Century, made his definition of our

1

unconscious minds, claiming that we share what he called a 'collective unconscious' which is inherited and is the same for all people. This collective unconscious contains a large number of what he called 'archetypes', which we will see correspond to earlier religions' panoply of different gods. We will also compare the Jewish and Christian perspectives on their monotheistic God to show that, whilst He may be claimed to be 'One God', His personality as shown in both Old and New Testaments of The Bible actually displays all the variety of the separate gods of the Greeks and Romans.

This collective unconscious, buried deep in every person's physical brain, is where, following Jung, I will claim God is to be found – whether as a distinct entity or as a unifying principle of humanity – and is ultimately where God has always been found in every religion. Which brings us to the question of how this God within us can be communicated with. Again, the answer I will propose has a long history and has applied to almost every civilisation we know of. Mechanisms were found which were claimed to show what 'the gods' – or God – wanted to tell us. These mechanisms came in many forms: consulting the Oracle at Delphi; dissecting many animals and birds to form an augury; Tarot cards; soothsayers; and the Chinese I Ching. Judaism and Christianity have followed the same route. In the Old Testament the prophets performed the duties of the oracle, and claimed to give God's message to his people. In the New Testament we have St Paul giving lists of 'gifts of the Spirit' – prophecy, speaking in tongues, discernment of various 'spirits' and so on. Every religion seems to advocate meditation and deprivation of the senses as a method of sinking into our unconscious, where God may be found. The particular method I will advocate is the I Ching.

There is a good reason for opting for the I Ching, (pronounced something like Yi Kung), which will take us into the realms of bio-chemistry and DNA, because there is a notable mathematical correspondence between the two which seems to me to be more than coincidental. We will explore this connection thoroughly, because I believe it gives at least a plausible explanation of why and how an arcane Chinese divination technique might actually allow us to reach into our unconscious, and so communicate with the God within us.

And because Western philosophy seems unable to accept that such divination could conceivably be possible, we will take a brief look at the conclusions of quantum mechanics which throws up even more counter-intuitive but scientifically proven facts. Not that two wrongs make a right, but that there may be a connection between the sub-atomic firing of neurons in the brain and the behaviour of sub-atomic photons in quantum experiments. It is a rather fine coincidence that Jung honed his theories in conversation and correspondence with one of the great quantum physicists, Wolfgang Pauli, and we will look in some detail at their psychic exploration using Pauli's prolific dream life.

At a U.S. Department of Defence news briefing in February 2002 Donald Rumsfeld famously coined the phrase *"there are known knowns; these are things that we know that we know. We also know there are known unknowns; that is to say we know there are some things we do not know. But there are also unknown unknowns, the ones we don't know we don't know."* He left out one crucial, logical corollary: **There are unknown knowns, things we know, but don't know that we know.**

I have used this logical extension of Rumsfeld's epigram as my title because it seems to sum up what has happened to our apprehension of God and our loss of contact with our unconscious minds over the last few millennia. The further back we go from civilisation the more we find our more primitive ancestors being aware of the irrational, the unconscious urges that drive people. Their gods were many and personified those urges. Some were benign, such as Athena for the Greeks, Diana for the Romans, Vishnu in Hinduism and Baldur for the Norsemen. Some were decidedly malignant – destroyers, tricksters, unreliable allies at best. For the Greeks, Zeus, and for the Romans, Jupiter, are chief among the gods, and both are gods of war. In Hinduism Shiva is the great destroyer, and in Norse mythology Odin holds the same brief. Many other unconscious urges find their gods in the old religions such as the trickster gods, the gods of love, of revenge, of the underworld – a life after death.

We will find ourselves searching for God in that very same unconscious sphere, and indeed the God we will find there will retain all those primitive aspects. We will start with Jung's thesis of the collective unconscious, seeing how precisely it synchronises with the earlier gods and with myth and legend down the ages.

Chapter summary

The book is built around Carl Jung's thesis that each person has an unconscious which is partially made up of individual material – repressed memories, forgotten childhood memories and so on – but is largely formed by what he calls the Archetypes. These are unconscious images from our pre-conscious past as a race, and he contends that they are common to all human beings, calling them our 'collective unconscious'.

PART ONE:

Chapter one explores some of these archetypes, drawing attention to those Jung regarded as most important. The Anima is the feminine side to every man, and its counterpart is the Animus in women. The Mother is the Earth-mother, the capable, dependable figure in the background, extending to the Madonna and child. The Trickster is a complex of the devil, the fool, the 'spanner-in-the-works' and so on. The Shadow is made up of all the parts of us we would rather not acknowledge. There are many archetypes, and their reality is that they stray into each other's territory. The problem is that, because they lurk in our unconscious, their action is irrational in that they make us act without conscious thought, and the actions they provoke are often malign and destructive – especially when they become 'collective', that is actions within a crowd, picking up on the same collectively unconscious archetype. Here lies the root of mob rule and warfare.

Chapter two introduces Jung's contention that religion is essential to mankind in order to give a peaceful outlet for the collective unconscious. We look at the ancient Greek and Roman gods to see how they personify many of the archetypes and at Jung's conclusion that all we can truly know of God is unconscious, dwelling in our collective archetypes. Wolfgang Pauli, the eminent quantum physicist makes his first appearance, and we look briefly at two of his many dreams which he and Jung discussed and analysed together. One of them illustrates Jung's certainty that four, rather than three, is the fundamental archetypal number, leading to his promotion of the idea of God as a quaternity, rather than a trinity – an idea we will return to in chapter three.

Chapter three ties these ideas together, hypothesising that God is indeed to be found in our unconscious, and that the quaternity Jung seeks is in the four nucleotides – Adenine, Thymine, Cytosine and Guanine – which combine to make the DNA present in all living things. We compare this image of God with the biblical account to see how well DNA and our archetypes fulfil the various Christian doctrines.

Chapter four investigates some of the many ways people use and have used to access their unconscious minds, from asceticism to meditation; hermitages to monasteries; yoga to transcendental meditation. The I Ching is put forward as a particularly valuable tool in this inward journey, and Jung's particular fondness for it is shown in his foreword to the English translation of Richard Wilhelm's seminal original German translation of the ancient texts. The case for the use of the I Ching has been enhanced by the discovery in the 1990s that its form, when written in an 8 x 8 matrix corresponding to the binary number matrix 0 to 63, is identical to the standard biochemical matrix of the 64 codons produced by DNA. We look first at a typical I Ching reading – on *Enthusiasm* – as an example.

We go on to investigate the 'nuts and bolts' of making an I Ching reading, and demonstrate some of the metaphors used to assist connection to our unconscious. Yin and yang, the idea of 'moving yin' and 'moving yang', the basic trigrams of the I Ching, and finally the full hexagrams with their degrees of change are introduced. By the end of the chapter you should have all you need to generate a reading, look it up in the literature, and contemplate how the reading unlocks an unknown known to help you understand and better deal with any given situation.

Chapter five looks at the range of metaphor used in both the I Ching and in our dreams which help unlock the images in our unconscious. In particular we look at a selection of Pauli's dreams as reported by Jung, and the archetypes they are felt to have revealed. We then look at Wilhelm's translation of the 'Ten Wings', purportedly composed by Confucius himself, to see how the metaphors in the I Ching match these archetypal dreams, leading to a full list of the metaphors covered in each trigram. Taking reading 36, *'Darkening of the light'* as an example we see how the use of metaphor reveals the unknown knowns deep in our unconscious. The chapter ends with an extensive covering of all the many ways the I Ching uses to approach the readings.

Chapter six concentrates on the degrees of change, investigating the complex and varied ways lines may be held to correspond to each other. So we look at firm and yielding lines, superior and inferior positions of lines, nuclear trigrams, King Wen's influence – seeing each line as a position in court – the 'Time' factor, the relationship between various lines, the numbers (6,7,8 or 9) attributed to each line, and the special nature of the sixth line. As an example we study the degrees of change available in the case of reading no. 50, *The Great Bowl.*

Chapter seven introduces a pictorial approach to DNA with a simplistic look at how it is formed, how it continually unzips, and how one of the two unzipped sections is split into codons, which generate amino acids and proteins to maintain, grow and heal our bodies. A critical part of this chapter then investigates the six different correspondences that exist between DNA and the hexagrams of the I Ching. This culminates in the production of an 8 x 8 table which is simultaneously the binary numbers from 0 to 63, the I Ching hexagrams laid out in the Old Family Order, and the table of the amino acids produced by the 64 codons, laid out in the standard way, with the groupings of amino acids exactly as they are in bio-chemical textbooks.

Chapter eight poses the question 'So what? Why should there be anything more than mathematical pleasure in finding such a correspondence? To help me with this critical question I consulted the I Ching itself, producing reading no. 46, *Pushing Upward.* Apart from the comfort it provided that the thesis was holding together, it also provided the key line 'To understand how a tree is contracted into a seed is to understand the future unfolding of the seed into a tree.' This speaks of DNA, and leads to the proposition that since our Archetypes are transmitted generation to generation by our DNA, just as are our physical attributes, and since the I Ching has precisely the same pattern as DNA when laid out in the most fundamental way possible – the counting numbers – then it may well be that the I Ching hexagrams are entangled with the Archetypes, and subject to a quantum mechanical requirement to appear together. The chapter recognises just how speculative this thesis is, and simply places it before others for consideration.

The chapter ends with the question: 'What is the implication of all this for an increasingly secular and atheistic world?'

PART TWO:

Chapter nine explains the various ways of accessing the I Ching – three coins, fifty yarrow sticks, or sixteen beads in a bag. Recognising the slight disparity between coins and yarrow sticks it suggests a way of tossing coins to mirror the yarrow sticks exactly.

Chapter ten looks at Jung's theory of synchronicity and the diagram produced jointly with Pauli to show how we need to factor complementarity into both our world view of space/time versus conservation of energy, and likewise into our view of causality versus synchronicity. We look at possible reasons for the lack of any explicit quantum ideas in his exposition, given that he was working with such a luminary as Pauli.

Chapter eleven then goes on to investigate how quantum physics might nevertheless have a bearing on synchronicity. We start with a brief exposition of the bizarre properties of sub-atomic particles – their complementary states of being both particle and wave – and then at the concept of quantum entanglement, which is a candidate for a possible explanation both of synchronicity and the efficacy of the I Ching.

Chapter twelve begins the process of studying the groups of hexagrams which correspond to groups of mRNA codons which all produce one amino acid to see if there is a common theme in these groups. This chapter deals with the four groups on the principal diagonal of the 8 x 8 table, and finds there is indeed a common theme for each group.

Chapter thirteen continues this process for the other groups of four, finding they too have common themes.

Chapter fourteen completes this process for the various groups of two hexagrams, the three hexagrams corresponding to the Stop codons and the single Start codon.

Part one

This first part of the book is concerned to present the premise that any appreciation we have of God takes place in our unconscious, not our rational, mind. To help support this premise we study Jung's thesis that all mankind shares a collective unconscious, which is transmitted in our DNA, and which contains 'archetypes' which affect our behaviour. Given this premise we move on to argue that all religions down the ages have worshipped a God or gods who/which mirror these archetypes in their personalities.

The main thrust from there is to get to the amazing correspondence between the grouping of the codons produced from our DNA and the 64 hexagrams of the ancient Chinese I Ching. It is this correspondence which, to my mind, justifies the use of the I Ching as a tool to help us access the archetypes – the Unknown Knowns – hidden in our unconscious, and so to converse with God. This requires an amateur understanding of the I Ching, of course, and also of the way in which DNA produces the codons which maintain and sustain life, and each chapter contributes to this understanding.

Chapter one

Jung's thesis of the Collective Unconscious

Carl Jung and Sigmund Freud first met in 1906. For the following seven years they met frequently and kept up an intense correspondence in which Jung formulated his understanding of the unconscious, defending his fledgling thesis against the conflicting theories of the much older Freud, who famously held that our unconscious is formed from repressed conscious feelings, mostly sexual in nature. Jung was prepared to accept the existence of a 'personal unconscious' which might indeed be very Freudian, but he was much more interested, both personally and as a practising psychiatrist, in what he called the 'collective unconscious'. He defined this thus:

"My thesis then, is as follows: in addition to our immediate consciousness, which is of a thoroughly personal nature and which we believe to be the only empirical psyche (even if we tack on the personal unconscious as an appendix), there exists a second psychic system of a collective, universal, and impersonal nature which is identical in all individuals. This collective unconscious does not develop individually but is inherited. It consists of pre-existent forms, the archetypes, which can only become conscious secondarily and which give definite form to certain psychic contents." C. G. Jung, *The Archetypes and the Collective Unconscious* (London 1996 edition) *p. 43, paragraph 90.*

This is the unconscious I have labelled the 'Unknown Knowns' which I believe the I Ching, the Chinese Book of Changes, can help us to access in particular situations where we will benefit from a deeper understanding than we can reach by rational, conscious thought alone. Note Jung's insistence that these unknown knowns are common to all people, of every race and creed. He asserts that they are in the deepest parts of our brain, the part we used as brute animals, long before we developed our astounding powers of conscious, rational thought. Inasmuch as they are by definition 'unconscious' we can only really experience them unconsciously, rather than express them consciously, but Jung developed his thesis of 'The Archetypes' as a way of attempting to understand what sorts of concepts are contained in this collective unconscious. These archetypes appear time and time again in the mythologies of every culture, from the cave drawings of prehistory to the gods and goddesses of Rome and Greece. E.R. Dodds, in his erudite *The Greeks and the Irrational (1951)* writes of the 'daemons' and gods who, in the Iliad and the Odyssey cause various heroes to act completely out of character, sometimes with disastrous results. This rather long quotation is worth giving in full for the insight it gives into the nature of the archetypes. "The most characteristic feature of the Odyssey is the way in which its personages ascribe all sorts of mental (as well as physical) events to the intervention of a nameless and indeterminate daemon or 'god' or 'gods'. These vaguely conceived beings can inspire courage at a crisis or take away a man's understanding, just as gods do in the Iliad. But they are also credited with a wide range of what may be called loosely 'monitions'. Whenever someone has a particularly brilliant or a particularly foolish idea; when he suddenly recognises another person's identity or sees in a flash the meaning of an omen; when he remembers what he might well have forgotten or forgets what he should have remembered, he or someone else will see in it, if we are to take the words literally, a psychic intervention by one of these supernatural beings." *(p 10-11)*. Jung would see in it the action of an archetype, stirring in the unconscious brain.

Arguably these archetypes form the basis of every religion – a theme we will return to later. Also, importantly, they appear woven into the 64 readings of the I Ching, which we will study in greater depth later in this book, as a tool to help us contact our own unconscious. Before we look at Jung's archetypes, here is a very brief introduction to the eight basic elements of the I Ching, which we will refer to frequently in connection with the archetypes.

THE EIGHT BASIC MOTIFS IN THE I CHING

Heaven: The creative, fatherly, masculine element.

Earth: The complementary mother figure.

Water: Standing variously for danger, persistence, and our deepest core – our soul.

Fire: Representing ambition, clinging to things, heated emotions.

Thunder: Energy, forcefulness, strength and shock.

Mountain: The ability to remain still, focused. The unmoved, eternal.

Wood or Wind: Interestingly these are paired, and stand for gentle but persistent penetration to the root of a problem.

Lake: Representing joy, fulfilment and capacity.

There is no definitive list of archetypes, and they tend to merge one into the other, but we will look in more detail at the seven Jung concentrated on most.

The Mother

A creature as helpless as we are for such a long time of childhood experiences (generally) its mother throughout its formative years. It is no surprise that the whole concept of motherhood should be an archetypal image for all humanity. At its most positive, the archetype brings feelings of being loved, nurtured, warm and cared-for; but if the reality falls short of this the obverse is an overbearing, suffocating, prescriptive presence that an adult actively seeks to throw off. Again, art and mythology abound with images. The Virgin Mary, the Madonna and Child, our mother country and so on represent the positive; the negative is often the evil stepmother or the terrifying vision in the New Testament book *'Revelations'*, *Ch 17 vs 3,4:* 'There I saw a woman sitting on a scarlet beast that was covered with blasphemous names and had seven heads and ten horns. The woman was dressed in purple and scarlet, and was glittering with gold, precious stones and pearls. She held a golden cup in her hand, filled with abominable things and the filth of her adulteries; and on her forehead was written a name of great mystery: Babylon the great, mother of harlots and of the earth's abominations.' In fact, Revelations is brim-full of archetypes of all kinds and is worthy of study specifically for this purpose.

The earliest Greek gods included Gaia, the 'earth mother' figure. Her Roman equivalent was Terra Mater (literally earth mother). Later, more developed mother goddesses include Hera for the Greeks and her Roman equivalent Juno (both married to the main male gods).

If a man suffers from an imbalance in this archetype he may display a mother-complex, projecting his need, for instance, to please his mother into his dealings with all women. A woman, on the other hand, may live her entire life for her children, or rebel against the whole syndrome and refuse motherhood. It becomes clear why mechanisms which reveal our hidden archetypes to us are so important. In discussing The Mother archetype Jung, perhaps unconsciously, makes it clear how closely the I Ching foreshadows his thesis. "The (mother) archetype is often associated with things and places standing for fertility and fruitfulness: the cornucopia, a ploughed field, a garden. It can be attached to a rock, a cave, a tree, a spring, a deep well, or to various vessels such as the baptismal font, or to vessel-shaped flowers like the rose or the lotus... Hollow objects such as ovens and cooking vessels are associated with the mother archetype, and, of course, the uterus, yoni, and anything of like shape. Added to this list there are many animals, such as the cow, hare, and helpful animals in general." (*op. cit., paragraph 156*)

Compare this to the list of the attributes of the Earth motif in the I Ching, which we will discuss later: *The Receptive is the earth, the mother. It is cloth, a kettle, frugality; it is level, a cow with a calf, a large wagon, form, the multitude, a shaft. Among the various kinds of soil it is the black.*

Main attribute: yielding. Associated animal: cow.

14

We will find parallels to all the archetypes in the 64 hexagrams of the I Ching, as we explore its use in unlocking our unknown knowns.

The Anima and Animus

Jung claims "I shall begin with a brief statement: in the unconscious of every man there is hidden a female personality, and in that of every woman a masculine personality." *(ibid, para 511)*

This is the fundamental archetype, the assertion that every trait contains within it the opposite trait. This is the starting point of Taoism – Yin and Yang – and we shall meet it many times in our exploration of the I Ching. We encounter the anima/animus in all the male-female pairs of deities: Ardhanarishvara in Hinduism; Hermaphroditus, son/daughter of Hermes and Aphrodite in Greek mythology or of Venus and Mercury in the Roman version; even, arguably, God the Father and God the Holy Spirit in Christianity. And so on. Even from his pre-DNA-mapping perspective Jung can recognise that male and female share the great majority of their genes in common, and so finds it inevitable that this hidden personality should be a basic archetype. The anima (for men) and animus (for women) appear frequently in dreams. The chief way psychiatrists recognise archetypes in clients is through their 'projections' – ascribing the archetypal images to a real person. When a man projects his archetypal image of 'woman', his anima, on to an actual woman he imbues her with all his fantasies of womanliness: she is beautiful beyond compare; he will die if he cannot have her; her wisdom is outstanding, and so on. And of course vice-versa for the animus in a woman. This projection can take many aberrant forms, leading to Don Juan-ism or nymphomania at one end of the scale and a Ruskin-like over-idealisation of the female at the other. One way or another, man's anima and woman's animus will lead them out of conscious 'good behaviour' into a form of madness in which the desired person becomes the overwhelming obsession of their lives. For a time.

In mythology and art the anima is often portrayed as a siren, a mermaid, or a goddess. Titian's *Diana and Acteon* expresses the idea

15

perfectly, as does its companion *Venus and Adonis*. Actual sex is quite absent: the anima as represented here is chaste. This is made explicit in his *Diana and Callisto*, where the pregnant Callisto is cast out from Diana's company.

Probably the earliest specific reference (around 400 BC) in Western philosophy to a concept mirroring that of the anima is Plato's exposition of the idea of 'Eros'. We have emasculated his philosophy by sloppy use of the phrase 'Platonic love', meaning little more than friendship between a man and a woman, explicitly non-sexual. Plato certainly included sexual attraction as part of Eros, but held that it meant much more than mere sex or friendship. "Eros also supplies the dynamic impulse which drives the soul forward in its quest of a satisfaction transcending earthly experience. It thus spans the whole compass of human personality, and makes the one empirical bridge between man as he is and man as he might be." (*Dodds, op. cit. p218*) Jung's definition of the archetypal anima/animus could be identically described.

In the I Ching there are eight fundamental motifs: the anima comes to light especially in readings including the Earth motif (*as above*), and the Water motif (*danger, among horses it means those with beautiful backs, those with wild courage, those which let their hair hang, those with thin hoofs, those which stumble*). The animus appears in readings containing the Heaven motif (*The Creative is heaven. It is round, it is the prince, the father, jade, metal, cold, ice; it is deep red, a good horse, an old horse, a wild horse, tree fruit. It is straight, it is the dragon, the upper garment, the word. Main attribute: strength. Associated animal: horse*) and the Thunder motif (*The arousing is thunder, the dragon. It is dark yellow, a spreading out, a great road, the eldest son. It is decisive and vehement; it is bamboo that is green and young, it is reed and rush. Among horses it signifies those which can neigh well, those with white hind legs, those which gallop, those with a star on the forehead. And among useful plants it is the pod-bearing ones. Finally, it is the strong, that which grows luxuriantly. Main attribute: movement. Associated animal: dragon.*)

You may well be thinking that the example from Revelations, above, of the whore on the beast sits more readily with the Anima archetype – and you may well be right. The reality is that many archetypes overlap: most readily those of the Mother and the Anima.

The Shadow

This is a slightly different archetype in that it coincides to some extent with the 'personal unconscious' and the Freudian concept of repressed memories. Like the anima, the shadow appears in much literature and mythology, spectacularly for instance in '*Dr. Jekyll and Mr Hyde*'. In Jung's description "the shadow personifies everything that the subject refuses to acknowledge about himself and yet is always thrusting itself upon him directly or indirectly – for instance inferior traits of character and other incompatible tendencies." *(op.cit., para 513.)* This is one I recognise very well in that as soon as I start to work with non-human entities – animals or inanimate – I begin to get angry and to swear quite against my better judgement and knowingly against optimum achievement. I suspect a great deal of road-rage is the same shadow archetype making its presence felt.

There are many Biblical examples of erstwhile heroes displaying their shadow sides. Much of the First and Second Books of Samuel applaud David, who became king by valour and integrity, but in *2 Samuel 11* we read how, as the great king, David first falls under the spell of his Anima as he becomes bewitched by the beautiful Bathsheba, and then gives in to his Shadow as he callously sends her husband Uriah off to certain death in his army, so that David may possess her. This example highlights the frequent pairing of Anima and Shadow. In the New Testament we see St Paul expressly recognise his shadow in *Romans 7: 15–17*. "I do not understand my own actions. For I do not do the thing that I want, but I do the very thing that I hate. Now, if I do what I do not want, I agree that the law is good. So then it is no longer I that do it, but sin which dwells within me."

In the I Ching, readings including the Water motif frequently help put us in touch with the Shadow. (*The abysmal is water, ditches, ambush, bending and straightening out, bow and wheel. Among men it means the melancholy, those with sick hearts, those with earache. It is the blood sign; it is red. Among horses it means those with beautiful backs, those with wild courage, those which let their hair hang, those with thin hoofs, those which stumble. Among chariots it means those with many defects. It is penetration, the moon. It means thieves. Among varieties of wood it means those which are firm and have much pith. Main attribute: dangerous. Associated animal: pig.)*

The Hero

The archetype perhaps most beloved of fairy-tales and the cinema. In some respects the hero transcends the unconscious, for the hero's chief feat is to defeat the terrors of darkness, and bring all into the light. This is in itself an archetype for the dawning of the conscious mind out of the pre-historic gloom of merely unconscious living. In the I Ching readings including the Thunder motif (*as above*) are often illustrative of the hero archetype.

Homer's 'The Odyssey' is, at base, a protracted exploration of the Hero archetype, as Odysseus struggles against many other archetypal figures eventually to reach home. Among them is Circe, the bewitching Anima figure, who turns his fellow-sailors into wolves, lions and swine, as is frequently the effect of a man's first contact with his anima. The hero figure is also often intertwined with the 'Old Man/Woman' or Sage archetype (see below), and Odysseus is no exception, frequently being helped out by the goddess Athena. Gandalf fulfils the same role for Bilbo Baggins in Tolkien's 'The Hobbit' and for Frodo in 'The Lord of the Rings.'

Fairy tales and legend abound with heroes, struggling and eventually prevailing against dark forces. Jack, of beanstalk fame, Cinderella, King Arthur, St. George – the list is endless. Religions too always have their heroes. The Old Testament revels in the exploits of King David, Moses, Saul and Jonathon while Christianity has focused more on its saints, facing persecution for their faith. For the Greeks, Achilles and Heracles stand out whilst the Romans deified their emperors.

The Child

Partly, this archetype stores in the unconscious all those memories of childhood that never made it into our conscious memory, but it is much more than that, or it would not be a 'collective' archetype. Jung puts it thus: "the child motif represents the pre-conscious, childhood aspect of the collective psyche." *(ibid, para 273.)* Its mythology and significance in many religions is formidable: child-gods abound, from the baby Jesus, through Cupid and the Egyptian Horus and on to the Greek Harpocrates. The one New Testament story virtually every Briton knows is that of the Nativity – even though its biblical provenance is only a half-chapter of Luke's Gospel *(Ch. 2:1-20)* and a rather different story in Matthew *(Ch. 2)*. Childhood is still a time of terrors and perplexity, a time when instinct (both the child's and its parents') holds sway, protecting, teaching and guarding. This has always been so and the child archetype is perhaps the one we all experience in our own infancy, before rational consciousness takes us over. Dreams of childhood, with all its terrors and uncertainties, are some of the most common. Six of the eight I Ching basic building blocks contain allusions to various child archetypes, amongst many other things.

The Trickster

This is perhaps an unexpected archetype: one might have thought pre-history too 'red in tooth and claw' to allow for buffoonery, but Jung is persuasive in his handling of the motif, devoting a full chapter *(ibid. paras 456 to 488)* to the concept. The trickster archetype appears in a bewildering array of fantasy, fairy tale, carnival, witchery and wizardry, myth and religious formats. Here belong the devil, poltergeists, all the superstitions about ladders and mirrors, Puck in A Midsummer Night's Dream, the bogeyman, Voodoo shaman, witch-doctor and many, many more. It is quite closely related to our 'shadow' archetype, both belonging to the areas of life where things go wrong and our reactions are poorer than strict consciousness would allow.

Particularly in religious life the trickster is a frequent figure. The Old Testament God seems frequently capricious, visiting death and destruction on the Israelites and their enemies in anything but a 'fair' way, and frequently applauding very underhand behaviour in his chosen people. The very first 'commandment' (Exodus 20: vs.4) contains the threat 'for I the Lord your God am a jealous God, visiting the sins of the father upon the children to the third and fourth generation of those who hate me'. Even in the New Testament there are parables and sayings of Jesus that belong in truth to this trickster archetype. Think of the parable of the unjust steward, or the demand to follow Jesus immediately, with no regard to father and mother, leaving 'the dead to bury their dead'.

Many cultures enact carnivals and the like where the character of the trickster is played out both by specified individuals but also in a joyous mass demonstration by the entire crowd. Thus, for instance, in Voodoo there is a particularly mischievous/devious/wicked shaman, but also the onlookers work themselves into a trance-like state and participate in every kind of mischief. Even here in prosaic Britain we maintain the last vestiges on 1st April, with April Fool's Day – a mere shadow of the mock masses allowed in the Catholic church of the Middle Ages when deliberate caricatures of the normal solemnity were enacted by all comers.

The wise old man/woman

It is easy to see how an image of elderly wisdom would hark back to pre-conscious pre-history. There are several examples in the animal kingdom where older beasts lead – to better pastures, to water, on the traditional migration routes – and we may speculate that as man became more conscious, using fire for instance, it would be the elders who knew and taught how it was done. As language developed and oral history became important, again it would be the old men and women who re-told the old stories to another generation. This archetype has lodged in our collective unconscious and emerges, as usual, in myth, legend and dream. King Arthur has his Merlin, Tolkien his Gandalf , and it is often true that the wise old man has a whiff of sorcery and wizardry about him. Socrates fulfils the role in Plato's writings, and the Old Testament resonates with the teaching of elderly prophets.

The I Ching reserves a special place for the sage in its readings, as we shall see when we look in detail at the readings themselves.

It is here, in what Jung insists is a shared, collective unconscious, that we will look for God. We have seen, briefly, how many earlier religions seem to have produced gods who conform to the archetypes Jung specifies as the inhabitants of our collective unconscious, and in that sense they too have found god here, in the guise of many different gods. This is not to argue that God is merely subjective, a product of our own imagination, for these archetypes, this collective unconscious, are common to all people, regardless of race or degree of civilisation. This is the place sought by those who meditate, who seek to banish conscious thought in order to reach their unconscious. In doing so, they are seeking out their unknown knowns. Meditation links Eastern and Western religions: the Hindu or Buddhist practising his yoga; the dervish dancing himself into a trance; the Christian anchorite walled up to keep out all external stimulus – all are excluding their conscious minds in order to contact this collective unconscious.

Jung is adamant that to be a truly rounded personality we need to try to bring these unconscious archetypes into our conscious realm – a process he terms 'Individuation' with a pun intended: in-dividuation = the state of not being divided, indivisible. That is, the personality is not separated into conscious and unconscious because the individual is aware of the unconscious forces within his brain. He is aware of the unknown knowns within him, and being aware makes him a more rounded being.

In Christian terms, this process is the equivalent of prayer. True prayer, in the Christian understanding, is a process of seeking to align ourselves with the 'will of God'. It should not be an attempt to alter God's will, to get Him on our side, or to change history in our favour. Rather, it should be an attempt to understand all points of view, to harness our energies for good, and to align ourselves with the 'right' way of being. There are many ways of praying, many ways of seeking to know God's will. In this book I will be advocating the use of the I Ching, partly because in practice I have found it a very useful aid to prayer, but particularly because its form mirrors what we now know of the structure of DNA. It is this very precise correspondence which convinces me that it is capable of directly contacting our unknown knowns, of putting us in touch with the collective unconscious which I am also convinced contains all we can truly know of God. When it does the results are not outlandish, bizarre or even really unexpected. The counsel in this remarkable set of readings is balanced, recognisable, and indeed should be instinctive, since it is drawn from these ancient archetypes that are our very foundations.

Chapter two

Religion and the collective unconscious

Carl Jung found a deep interpenetration between religion and his concept of the collective unconscious – in particular the Catholic church's version of religion. In his Terry Lectures, delivered to Yale University in 1937/8 he developed his thoughts on the interplay between Psychology and Religion, published as a booklet of the same name in 1938 – in the shadow of the looming WWII. He begins with a defence of the psyche as a reality outside our imaginings, using the example of a man convinced he has a cancer, even though he 'knows' in his rational mind that he has not. His distress is all the greater because he feels it is his own fault: his neurosis is somehow of his own making. Jung is at pains to defend the absolute reality of the psyche, and of the archetypes which lurk within it. He even tells his patient that he does indeed have a cancer, not in his physical body but in his unconscious, and that if not treated by bringing it out into the open and possibly inflicting radical 'surgery' on it the cancer will indeed kill his psyche, and hence his body too.

He goes on to observe that since these archetypes are collective they are much stronger in a collective atmosphere, when people congregate together for whatever reason. Probably with the worsening situation in Germany in mind he warns of the danger of these destructive archetypes taking over when a crowd gathers. A crowd quickly becomes a mob. This is certainly borne out in our own experience. Men (and women) do terrible things in mobs that they would control as individuals. Football crowds, music festivals, demonstrations and particularly warfare unleash forces that we are unwilling to admit dwell within us. But they do, as the darker archetypes and the rise of Nazism in Germany were making clear. Throughout this little booklet Jung sees more danger in our collective unconscious, and more need to bring the archetypes under some control, than he expresses in all the rest of his writings.

The body he sees as chiefly able to offer this control is the church, and in particular the Catholic church. Recognising the immense psychic power available to crowds and organised groups of people the Catholic church, he claims, has firstly harnessed it for creativity, in the building of huge cathedrals and smaller churches in every community; and secondly has established rites, doctrines and sacraments to defuse and give expression to this potent psychic force within each of us. Confession, Absolution and the Mass; art, symbolism and sacrament all conspire to shield the congregation from what, in this booklet, Jung sees as the darker forces in our collective unconscious.

He contrasts the Catholic church with its dogma, rites, and offer to allow individuals to be absolved of their 'sins' – their giving in to darker forces – with the Protestant churches which he sees as toothless in the face of the collective unconscious precisely because they have given up the rites, the doctrines, the papal infallibility in favour of each person's personal experience of God. In this he, perhaps unconsciously, is following the line first established by Plato some 2,300 years earlier. To quote again from E R Dodds: 'He (Plato) felt however the need for something like a church, and a canon of authorised rituals, if religion was to be prevented from running off the rails and becoming a danger to public morality. In the field of religion, as in that of morals, the great enemy which had to be fought was antinomian individualism; and he looked to Delphi to organise the defence. We need not assume that Plato believed the Pythia (the Oracle of Delphi) to be verbally inspired. My own guess would be that his attitude to Delphi was more like that of a modern "political Catholic" towards the Vatican: he saw in Delphi a great conservative force which could be harnessed to the task of stabilising the Greek religious traditions and checking both the spread of materialism and the growth of aberrant tendencies within the tradition itself.' *(The Greeks and the irrational, pp 222-3)*

In all this, as with his defence of the psyche as a reality because it is experienced as such, Jung sees God as a reality and religion as a valid activity because their effect on our unconscious is undeniable. For Jung it is an irrelevant question as to whether God 'exists' in some plane: he exists in our collective unconscious and the archetypes we all share, and we are all affected by this unconscious whether we be atheists or of any of the world religions. We will soon have a closer look at the archetypes as expressed in religion, in particular in Christianity, but before we leave Jung's book on Psychology and Religion we will take note of his exposition of two of Wolfgang Pauli's dreams about religion.

A SERENDIPITOUS FRIENDSHIP

Wolfgang Pauli was among the pre-eminent Quantum physicists of the 1920s and 30s. The Pauli Exclusion principle bears his name, and it was he who in 1930 demonstrated mathematically that there must be a fourth fundamental particle, to go alongside the electron, the proton and the neutron. He called it the neutrino. It was a further 26 years before his mathematics were vindicated by its discovery in the laboratory. Pauli now lived near Zurich, fortunately just two stations down the line from Carl Jung's mansion at 228 Seestrasse, Küsnacht, also near Zurich. Fortunate on two scores: mainly, from our point of view, because their friendship, letters and late-night conversations generated many psychological insights, but also because Pauli's non-scientific life was dragging him into psychological destitution.

A Jekyll and Hyde character, Pauli, the eminent, hard-working and inspired physicist by day, had spent many of his nights in the notorious seedy nightclubs of Hamburg, drinking and whoring, much to his self-disgust. Well-aware of his famous psychiatrist neighbour he sought help in his crisis, and their first meetings were as doctor and potential patient. (In fact, Jung didn't take on Pauli's psychoanalysis, but referred him to a colleague and student of his, Erna Rosenbaum. It seems Jung preferred to have Pauli as a friend and collaborator, and perhaps felt the Doctor/Patient relationship would compromise this.) It was 1932, Pauli was 31, Jung 57: their decades-long friendship and cross fertilisation bore fruit in the field of quantum physics where Pauli was able to use Jung's psychological insights to feel his way to a deeper understanding of the fourth quantum number, an understanding beyond the narrow boundaries of science using instead Jung's 'archetypes'. For his part, Jung was able to tap into Pauli's scientific and highly original mind, and in particular his dreams, to anchor his theories on the psyche on a firmer footing.

PAULI'S RELIGIOUS DREAMS

Pauli was a lapsed Catholic, an outstandingly brilliant physicist who suffered from a very skewed personality. His capacity to feel emotion was stunted in the utmost; overshadowed by the complementary thinking mode. As a rational scientist he had no time for religion, but by 1932 his unconscious was threatening his very sanity, with his anima in particular screaming to be recognised. As mentioned above, Jung refused actually to be his analyst, preferring instead to correspond with him as a friend, gathering and helping to analyse his prolific dream life. Two of those dreams were about religion specifically, and Jung spends a lot of his Terry Lecture time on them – without of course at that time revealing that Pauli was the subject.

This is not the place to give the full text of the dream, although Jung does so in his lecture. In brief Pauli dreams he enters a house which proclaims itself 'the universal Catholic church' with a friend, who wonders why the crowd needs to gather together in order to have religious feelings. Pauli replies "You are a protestant so you will never understand it." There is a woman who nods approval at this.

Inside is based on the Hagia Sophia, a famous Greek Orthodox church in Istanbul, turned mosque and now museum, with a wonderful effect of spaciousness. There are no images, but there are framed sentences on the wall, one of which reads 'Do not flatter your benefactor'. The same woman begins to weep at this and says

"Then there is nothing left at all." Pauli replies "I think that is perfectly all right," but she vanishes.

There is a great crowd of believers, but Pauli is the outsider, standing alone. They say together, "We confess that we are under the power of the Lord. The kingdom of heaven is within ourselves," – and later "Everything else is paper." The service, if that is what it is, breaks up and becomes instead something of a party, with wine and food and a sort of Epicurean meandering chatter, as a celebration that a new member – Charlie – has been enrolled. A priest explains rather apologetically that they are having to accommodate to big crowds and must therefore adopt some American methods. But he is anxious to stress that unlike the Americans 'we cherish an emphatically anti-ascetic tendency'. Pauli wakes with a feeling of great relief.

Jung draws several lessons from this dream. Firstly, it favours the Catholic church because of its traditions of togetherness, solemnity and rite. The Protestant view that religion is an individual experience is discouraged here. The second, to him 'more grotesque part', regards the church's adaptation to a worldly point of view, with feasting and 'anti-asceticism'. Jung has great difficulty with this modernism. In both parts of the dream the importance of crowds is emphasised, and Jung comments that Pauli apparently feels no opposition to collective feeling, mass religion or paganism. And then we come to the woman.

Pauli had already frequently dreamt of her, and Jung is in no doubt she represents his deeply-buried Anima archetype: in many ways the root of Pauli's malaise. Interestingly the name shares the same root as 'animosity', and true to type the anima in men, and animus in women, cause illogical moods, irritating topics of conversation and unreasonable opinions. Her wholly negative reactions in the church dream shows how Pauli's unconscious feminine side disagrees with his attitude. Pauli, as dreamer, agrees with the sentiment "Do not flatter your benefactor." Indeed, his history is littered with examples of his aggressive put-downs such as his public comment to a lecture crowd addressed by Einstein: "Actually, his ideas are not as stupid as you might think!" His feeling anima knows he oversteps the mark, and shrinks from him.

TRINITY OR QUATERNITY?

Paul's second overtly religious dream is very specific, and full of symbolism. Here is the entire text as related in *Psychology and Religion* *(page 42)*.

"I am in a solemn house. It is called 'the house of inner composure or self-recollection.' In the background are many burning candles arranged so as to form four pyramid-like points. An old man stands at the door of the house. People enter, they do not talk and often stand still in order to concentrate. The old man at the door tells me about the visitors to the house and says: 'When they leave they are pure'. I enter the house now, and am able to concentrate completely. A voice says: 'What thou art doing is dangerous. Religion is not a tax which thou payest in order to get rid of the woman's image, for this image is indispensable. Woe to those who use religion as a substitute for the other side of the soul's life. They are in error and shall be cursed. Religion is no substitute, but is the ultimate accomplishment added to every other activity of the soul. Out of the fullness of life thou shalt give birth to thy religion, and only then shalt thou be blessed.' Together with the last sentence a faint music becomes audible, simple tunes played on an organ, reminding me somewhat of Wagner's 'fire magic' (Feurzauber). As I leave the house I have the vision of a flaming mountain and I feel that a fire which cannot be quenched must be a sacred fire."

Here we have several archetypes – plus the unconscious use of archaic language for a religious dream. The old man, as usual, is the sage, wise old man archetype, and more interestingly the Anima is here again, refusing to allow Pauli to ignore her and to suppress the feminine, feeling side of his nature. The fire on the mountain leads me inevitably to the I Ching reading no. 56 'The Wanderer (The Seeker)', whose image is 'fire on a mountain'. Pauli is the epitome of the seeker, delving deep into the mysteries of quantum mechanics, but here in his meetings with Jung is honestly seeking his own salvation, knowing the depths of depression that led him there. Had they followed up the I Ching reading Pauli would have found sound advice in The Judgement, part of which reads 'When a man is a wanderer he should not be gruff or overbearing, nor give himself airs.' There is no evidence that they did.

Jung draws attention to the voice which, as he explains, is a regular feature of Pauli's dreams. It frequently issues a statement – as in this instance – which is clear and convincing, though often at odds with Pauli's conscious opinions. Jung goes on to observe that in Pauli's case, as in the cases of many of his patients, the voice issuing precise statements is 'an important and even decisive representation of the unconscious' *(ibid. p 45)*.

However, the symbol Jung seizes on and spends many pages exploring is that of the candles at the very beginning of the dream – because they are arranged to form four pyramid-like points. He and Pauli spent a great deal of their time together dwelling on the numbers three and four, including complex expositions of medieval alchemy which apparently put great emphasis on these numbers. It is enough for our purposes to consider the Christian perspective of these numbers, which Jung does at great length. He observes that the basic Christian symbol is the Trinity, but argues that this is in conflict with the collective unconscious which would see four as the fundamental number, and does so in many of Pauli's dreams. Pauli, as mentioned, first made his name by requiring that the atom, previously regarded as having three elements – proton, neutron and electron – must in fact have four, adding the neutrino to maintain conservation of energy.

Jung points out that the accepted Trinity – Father, Son and Holy Spirit – is psychologically unbalanced on several counts: counts which the collective unconscious will not accept, and insists on requiring a quaternity. There are four basic elements: earth, water, fire and air. For millennia we understood ourselves to be composed of four 'humours', black bile, yellow bile, phlegm and blood – leading to the four basic human characterisations of being melancholic, choleric, phlegmatic or sanguine. In I Ching terms the Trinity contains Heaven = Father, Water = Son and Fire = Holy Spirit; but is lacking the fundamental Earth = Mother figure. Jung observes that Catholicism, recognising the imbalance in the Trinity, quietly evened it up to the psychologically necessary four by elevating the Virgin Mary to a position alongside the Trinity. She was the needed feminine, earth quality that was missing.

These examples are of course all Christian, which is the only religion I know much about, but Jung knew many more and assures us the Quaternity is at the base of them all – because it is one of the archetypes in our global collective unconscious. He sums it all up thus: "We might, therefore, conclude that the symbol (the number four), spontaneously produced in the dreams of modern people, means the same thing – *the God within*." (His italics.) *(ibid. page 72)*

Jung knew nothing of DNA, nor of the four basic nucleotides that do indeed combine to form all life, and are arguably indeed *the God within*. I wish he had, for where might he and Pauli have gone with such knowledge?

Before we go on to ponder just that, I must acknowledge Jung's own caveat on psychology and religion: "It would be a regrettable mistake if anybody should understand my observations to be a kind of proof of the existence of God. They prove only the existence of an archetypal image of the deity, which to my mind is all we can assert psychologically about God. But as it is a very important and influential archetype, its relatively frequent occurrence seems to be a noteworthy fact for any 'theologia naturalis'" (Arguments for the existence of God from nature and observation rather than any revelation). *(ibid p. 73)*

Chapter three

The God within

Just as Jung felt it important to stress that his observations of the psychological apprehensions of spiritual reality were not to be taken as any proof of the objective reality of God, but only of the subjective reality of the archetypes in our collective unconscious, so I feel the need to affirm that in this chapter I am not seeking to prove God doesn't exist. However, it is my contention that all our spiritual experience is better explained by reference to our DNA and our collective unconscious and the archetypes therein than by any mystical spirituality. I shall largely restrict my observations to Christianity as that is the only religion I know well, though I have little doubt they would apply equally to any other religion or form of spiritual awareness.

QUATERNITY, DNA AND THE I CHING

As Jung observed the number four is actually the fundamental religious archetype, appearing in dreams and meditations the world over. The Christian Trinity is an artificial construct, missing the critical 'earth' motif that rightly belongs there. He is so excited by this that he proclaims (above) "We might, therefore, conclude that the symbol (the number four), spontaneously produced in the dreams of modern people, means the same thing – *the God within*." (His italics.)

Had he and Pauli been younger men when Watson and Crick made their great breakthrough in 1953, identifying the four nucleotides Adenine (A), Thymine (T), Cytosine (C) and Guanine (G) that combine so simply to make all life, I can only imagine the excitement it would have caused them. Here at the very heart of life, is the Quaternity Jung yearned for, the God within. Look at how this quaternity performs the very actions claimed for God in Genesis.

Genesis 1:11. And God said "Let the earth put forth vegetation, plants yielding seed and fruit trees yielding fruit in which is their seed, each according to their own kind, upon the earth." All actually were made from the quaternity ATCG – *the God within.*

Genesis 1:20. And God said "Let the waters bring forth swarms of living creatures, and let birds fly above the earth across the firmament of the heavens." All from the quaternity ATCG – *the God within.*

Genesis 1:24. And God said, "Let the earth bring forth living creatures according to their kinds… and it was so." All from the quaternity ATCG– *the God within.*

All forms of life are made from the fundamental four nucleotides ATC & G. No wonder the number four is such an important archetype: it is more than hard-wired into our unconscious; it is our very essence. I don't know whether DNA is somehow produced by an all-seeing external God, but together DNA and our collective unconscious do seem to fit Jung's vision of *'the God within'* remarkably snugly.

- One of Christianity's claims for God is that He is 'immanent', which is defined as being intimately involved with and sustaining all His creation. There can be no deeper immanence that that of DNA, which creates new individual lives continuously and actively sustains each life for its period on earth, and sustains also the archetypes that inhabit the unconscious of every human being.
- Christianity claims God as a 'person' in the sense that 'He' is interested in each of us as an individual, and that we can in some sense contact 'Him'. Our collective unconscious, the same in each of us, performs this action of God perfectly. We all have a share of this huge internal store of Unknown Knowns, and are intimately connected to it and to each other through it.
- God is proclaimed as Creator, Father. At least in terms of life, this is certainly true of DNA.

As St Paul says, 'we see through a glass darkly' – for they are our <u>unknown</u> knowns. But inasmuch as we do connect with the collective unconscious we do at least see a little of that vast store present in each of us. I can think of no better a description of God – at least in his dealings with mankind.

To demonstrate how the archetypes within our collective unconscious do indeed demonstrate the same truths as the teachings of the various religions, it will be instructive to compare its insights with those of Christianity.

Monotheism

Like Judaism and Islam, Christianity acknowledges only one God. I believe this is a deep-level recognition of the one-ness of the DNA which connects us all with all living things, and of the commonality Jung claims for our unconscious. The Old Testament contains many references to God's 'jealousy' of his uniqueness. Here are a couple of examples:

- You shall not make for yourself any graven image, or any likeness of anything that is in heaven above or on the earth beneath, or that is in the waters under the earth; you shall not bow down to them or serve them; for I the Lord your God am a jealous God, visiting the sins of the father's on their children to the third and fourth generation. [The second commandment] *(Exodus 20:5)*
- The Lord your God is a jealous God, a devouring fire. *(Deut. 4:24)*
- If you forsake the Lord and serve other Gods, then He will turn and do you harm, and consume you, after having done you good. *(Joshua 24:20)*

We are in a very real sense all one; linked by a common DNA and by Jung's collective unconscious. Of course our god should be 'one god'.

The Virgin Birth (and other miraculous births)

This is not actually a particularly strong element of the New Testament, appearing only in Luke's Gospel; but it is instructive to see what a hold it has gained on popular Christianity, being raised to an element of the creed. It is a strong metaphor, reflected in other religions, and should alert us to one of those unknown knowns. In this case, I think, the knowledge that inheritance matters. Long before we knew the details of DNA we knew instinctively that our ancestors mattered, signified in our make-up – physical, mental, emotional, intellectual, musical, artistic and personality. Many primitive religions focus on ancestor worship, moved by that same archetype. What could be more natural than a metaphor – virgin birth – to illustrate that Jesus shared both human and divine characteristics.

It is a metaphor shared with many other religions.

- In Hinduism, the divine Vishnu implanted himself in the womb of Devaki and was born as Krishna.
- The most popular legendary account of the birth of Buddha is in the Nidanakatha Jataka which accounted for the lives of Buddha in previous incarnations. In this account, the "Great Being" chose the time and place of his birth, the tribe into which he would be born, and who his mother would be. In the time chosen by him, Maya, his mother, fell asleep and dreamed that four archangels carried her to the Himalayan Mountains where their queens bathed and dressed her. In her dream the Great Being soon entered her womb from her side, in the form of a white elephant. When she woke, she told her dream to the Raja, who summoned sixty-four eminent Brahmans to interpret it. (Another connection to the sixty-four hexagrams?)
- In Judaism Moses, while not born to a virgin, has a miraculous escape from Pharaoh's clutches, in a story that resonates with Mary and Joseph's flight into Egypt to escape the wrath of Herod. Abraham's wife, Sara, is well beyond child-bearing age when she

conceives Isaac, thus providing the continuity of the nascent race. And even John the Baptist is born of Mary's relation Elizabeth, who was said to be barren.

Resurrection

This is an archetypal unknown known. It is true in a fundamental way that each of us does live on after death, in the sense that, if we have children, they carry on the DNA, the carrier of life, the 'living filament' that links us all. It is true in some very real senses that the 'resurrected Christ' lives on: his teaching, his parables, his example have affected the lives of billions of people over the last two millennia. His picture of God as 'Our Father' again, on the physical plane, recognises the over-arching life-giving force that is DNA. On the spiritual/unconscious plane it affirms every individual's worth and right to be here every bit as much as all other evolutions of DNA. Inasmuch as we all share the unconscious collectively, of course, there is a very real sense in which it is Father to us all, and that that aspect of our lives – a very real aspect – lives on after our death. Only our conscious mind, and the body that houses it, die. Our DNA and our unknown knowns go on.

This is not as appealing to our egos as the thought that maybe 'the essential me' lives on in some heaven, continuing to act and react with those we have loved, but it is easy to see that it may well be 'father to the wish'. The archetype behind the notion of some sort of life after death – resurrection, re-incarnation, heaven – is a reality.

The Trinity

Christianity has struggled with the concept of 'God the Holy Trinity' from its earliest days. The problem seems to me to be one of mistaken identity. The early church fathers felt the urge of an archetype – the quaternity – but instead of allowing the archetype free rein they rationalised it, forcing a collectively unconscious image into a conscious expression of dogma that didn't fit. In trying myself to express the archetype consciously I may well fall into the same trap, but let us try anyway. Actually, the early church soon recognised the problem and applied its own solution: to elevate the Blessed Virgin Mary to her rightful place as the fourth member of the Trinity – thereby turning it into the quaternity it should always have been. The Roman Catholic church has wisely kept this unconscious balance: the protestant churches, in their laudable but ultimately doomed insistence on making the irrational rational, have demoted Mary and so lost one of the crucial archetypes. God the Holy Quaternity makes good rational sense as well as fitting the archetype so well. Here we have Father, Mother, Son and, if we make the Holy Spirit so, daughter, or perhaps Wise old sage. The symbol is now balanced, satisfying, and a genuine light shone on an unknown known.

Atonement and sacrifice

The fundamental Christian insight is that Jesus' death should be seen as a sacrifice, an atonement for the sins of mankind. This presents the church with a difficult problem, never, to my mind at least, satisfactorily answered. As soon as we apply rationality to the concept, we are caught between Scylla and Charybdis. Scylla is a rock shoal on the mainland side of the straits of Messina, between Italy and Sicily. Charybdis is a whirlpool on the Sicily side of the straits. For the crucifixion, to describe it as a sacrifice brings us crashing onto Scylla's rocks – for to whom are we sacrificing? To be required to sacrifice God's son to placate God himself makes no rational sense. On the other hand, to see the crucifixion as Jesus' willing self-immolation 'to atone for the sins of us all' steers us into the whirlpool of Charybdis. Round and round we go. If God created us, why do we sin? If it is to give us freedom, what makes us choose evil? In any case, whence comes evil in a good God's creation?

Accept instead that we are at the mercy of our collective unconscious, a hotchpotch of urges, impulses and archetypes gathered over 200,000 years of being human, and there is no difficulty in understanding evil, sacrifice, or atonement. We are individually at the mercy of our Anima, our Shadow, the Trickster,

36

and so on: collectively we are in perpetual danger of an outburst such as Nazism or the Islamic State. And so, collectively, we have invented ways of purging our communities of these powerfully negative forces. The collective acts of ritual sacrifice, ritual scapegoating, make perfect sense, for they act on the same unconscious plane as do the negative archetypes themselves. It seems Jesus understood this perfectly well, as he instructed his disciples at the Last Supper to re-enact his self-sacrifice metaphorically and ceremonially in shared communion services with the words "Take, eat, for this is my body, given for you. This is my blood, shed for you; drink this in remembrance of me."

This collectively unconscious act will not accept rationalisation. The Catholic Church's insistence on the doctrine of transubstantiation in the 16th Century (the insistence that the wine was literally changed into the blood of Christ) was one of the many features of Christianity at that time which paved the way for Protestantism. The deeper meaning of the sacrament of communion – indeed any of the sacraments – can only be appreciated unconsciously: felt, not thought out. This is in no way to diminish its importance: our collective unconscious is fundamental to us as a people, and if we do not find and exercise ways of allowing its expression we wither and fall prey to all sorts of collective neuroses.

Saint Paul's theology

It is at least arguable that without Paul there would be no Christianity, for it was he who almost single-handedly elevated Jesus's actions to the level of archetypes, and so provided a religion that could satisfy people's need to celebrate their collective unconscious. The Last Supper, as shown above, provides the central action which Christians have celebrated for two thousand years. The words above are not recorded in John's gospel at all, and are not given as a template for repetition in or Matthew, Mark or Luke. The only time we get the command to repeat the action in remembrance of Jesus's sacrifice is in Paul's First Letter to the Corinthians, ch 11, vs 23 – 26. Here the need for repetition is made clear.... "Do this *as often as you drink it*, in remembrance of me. For as often as you eat this bread and drink this cup, you proclaim the Lord's death until he comes (again)." Here Paul commends a collective action which allows a congregation to access together an archetype: in this case a sacrifice. The archetype is reinforced in the last book of the bible – Revelations. Here Jesus is repeatedly referred to as 'the lamb of God' with all the overtones of sacrifice implied.

Paul it is, also, who generates the associated idea of atonement when he writes to the Christians in Rome "While we were still weak, at the right time Christ died for the ungodly. Why, one would hardly die for a righteous man – though perhaps for a good man one might dare even to die. But God shows his love for us in that while we were yet sinners Christ died for us. Since, therefore, we are now justified by his blood, much more shall we be saved by him from the wrath of God." *(Romans 5: 6-9)*. This is not meant to be rationalised, it is meant to be assimilated and recognised as the scapegoat archetype that it is. It is meant to find expression in an act of collective worship, to allow our unconscious to inform our lives.

Justification by faith alone is another distinctively Pauline philosophy – angrily refuted by the Letter of James, who sees faith without corresponding good works as a dead concept. James has not realised, as Paul has, that faith is, by definition, an archetypal attribute. Because faith means belief in something unprovable it is inherently irrational and appeals to the unconscious. Faith is a building block of religion, and it is largely thanks to Paul that it is incorporated in Christianity. Good works should indeed follow faith, and give outward expression to the beliefs of a religion, but it is the faith behind which actually belongs in the collective unconscious and is the strength of the religion.

In the beginning was the Word...

Perhaps the biggest parable of them all is this superb start to St. John's Gospel, worth quoting in full. "In the beginning was the Word, and the Word was with God, and the Word was God. He was in the beginning with God; all things were made through him, and without him was not anything made that was made. In him was life, and the life was the light of men. The light shines on in the darkness, and the darkness has not overcome it." *John 1: 1-5*

'Word' as used in this context is a translation of the Greek 'Logos', which has a much more complex meaning. It traces its roots back to Heraclitus (ca. 535-475 BC), who used the term for a principle of order and knowledge, and it became a technical term in philosophy. Of course, I am tempted to equate it with the unconscious, the unknown knowns, and to claim that this 'Logos/Word' is in truth all we know of God, and may indeed be God, whatever that might mean.

John goes on, a little further into the first chapter, to claim: "And the Word became flesh, and dwelt among us, full of grace and truth; and we have beheld his glory, glory as of the only Son of the Father." *John 1:14.* Yes indeed: if, as is my premise throughout, the I Ching and our DNA are intimately related, being identical in pattern, then it is not pushing the metaphor too far to say that the Word – the unconscious – became flesh, as DNA produces all life that ever was. And inasmuch as the I Ching allows us access to that unconscious, it is indeed the light of men.

John's other 'parables'

These are actually metaphorical claims he ascribes to Jesus, and it's easy to see how these could just as well be ascribed to our great, joint unconscious. These are the seven 'I am' sayings of Jesus, as recorded only in John's gospel. Three of these 'I am' sayings seem designed mainly to establish that Jesus has always been, always existed, as part of, or Son of, God. These are:

Again Jesus spoke to them, saying, **"I am** the light of the world. Whoever follows me will never walk in darkness but will have the light of life." *John 8:12*

Jesus said to him, **"I am** the way, and the truth, and the life. No one comes to the Father except through me." *John 14:6*

Jesus said to her, **"I am** the resurrection and the life. Those who believe in me, even though they die, will live." *John 11:25*

These are of a piece with John's first momentous claim, equating Jesus with the Logos, and I have no difficulty in going on to equate them with DNA/the unconscious, which ties us all together. It seems superfluous to go through the equations: the parallels are clear enough.

Why does John make these claims for Jesus in particular? I suppose in order to give us a personification of what is otherwise, perhaps, a rather dry concept – though to me, a vastly exciting one. I can only say that the glimpses of eternity, of God, that Christian worshippers find in Jesus, I find in communication, via the I Ching, with what I firmly believe is indeed a great unconscious, common to us all, shared by us all. I don't suppose it matters much how we apprehend it, as long as we are aware that there is much more to life than the merely physical here and now.

The other four 'I am' sayings in John are more parabolic, comparing Jesus to physical things in order to make a spiritual point. These are:

Jesus said to them, "**I am** the bread of life. Whoever comes to me will never be hungry, and whoever believes in me will never be thirsty." *John 6:35*

I am the gate/door; Whoever enters by me will be saved. *John 10:9*

I am the good shepherd. The good shepherd lays down his life for the sheep. *John 10: 11*

I am the true vine, and my Father is the vine grower. *John 15:1*

It will be no surprise to you that once again I have no difficulty ascribing the same metaphors to our unconscious/DNA, and to the I Ching as an unfailing guide. It is a 'gateway', an open door, into our unconscious, and that unconscious does indeed feed us, giving us sustenance, water, wine, what have you, in a spiritual sense.

Faith and belief

By definition, faith and belief refer to things we feel are true in some sense, but which cannot be proved rationally. Is this not just another way of saying 'things which are our unknown knowns?' We know deep in our unconscious that our religious feelings have an important meaning for us, and in that sense they are known. But they are not provable by any conscious rational process, and in that sense they are unknown. It is pointless for atheists such as Richard Dawkins to use rationality to mock and deride Christianity or any other religion. By all means point out the folly of those Christians who themselves try to rationalise their Christianity, taking the Bible as literal truth, as somehow the 'word of God'. Creation in the literal Genesis formulae is demonstrably ludicrous; but in a metaphorical sense, appealing to our unconscious, it is perfectly defensible. The many facets of God in the Bible or the Koran can easily be attacked if one has a simplistic picture of a 'loving father' figure; but not if one recognises that the biblical picture generally represents God in all the diversity of the archetypes in our collective unconscious.

If, instead of saying the doctrinaire Creed: "I believe in God the Father Almighty, maker of heaven and earth: and in Jesus Christ his only son, our Lord, who was conceived by the Holy Ghost, born of the virgin Mary, suffered under Pontius Pilate, was crucified, dead and buried: he descended into hell; the third day he rose again from the dead; he ascended into heaven, and sitteth on the right hand of God the Father Almighty; from thence he shall come to judge the living and the dead. I believe in the Holy Ghost; the holy Catholic Church; the communion of saints; the forgiveness of sins; the resurrection of the body, and the life everlasting. Amen."....

.... We were to say "I believe we have a collective unconscious which we all share, and which shapes our lives individually, collectively and nationally. I believe we need, individually, collectively and nationally to recognise, respond to, and honour this unconscious and its promptings. And I believe in the power of this unconscious to affect our lives, individually, collectively and nationally for both good and ill."… then our words would genuinely express a belief – an unconscious reality – not a conscious doctrine to be applied mercilessly in some periods of history.

Jung reminds us that these archetypes in our collective unconscious are not necessarily benign, and many religions picture a God or gods who can be fickle, jealous, vindictive and blood-thirsty. Christianity may have purged most of this from the New Testament, but the God of the Old Testament displays all those characteristics – not surprisingly if the archetypes are our only point of contact. As mentioned previously, giving the Terry Lectures on Psychology and Religion in 1937/8 Jung was only too conscious of the evil forces gathering in nearby Germany. Precisely because the unconscious is collective, these forces absorbed millions willingly into the ranks of Nazism, carried along by an internal, overwhelming power. Jung is convinced it is the task of religion to channel the collective unconscious for good purposes, to combat the potential for evil, and he is adamant that Catholicism in the West has managed this task well with its pomp and ceremony, confession and absolution.

Certainly Catholicism has preserved the harder side of God's nature far more than many Protestant offshoots. In the twentieth century the Church of England, in particular, has majored on a God of Love and swept most of Christianity's harsher aspects under a very English carpet. In its everyday dealings, even if not in its 39 articles, it presents forgiveness, charity, good-neighbourliness and 'Do unto others as you would they should do unto you'. This is partly admirable, but unfortunately ignores much of the unconscious that lurks in each of us, and so fails to either address it or give us a collective, crowd-friendly means of dealing with these base instincts.

There is of course in each service 'The General Confession'. If it were taken seriously it would indeed square up to the many self-centred anti-social archetypes within us, and then the Absolution might really mean something. But it is not. If the Anglican church took the doctrine of Atonement seriously its congregations would be brought face to face with the real cost of evil – and some intimation of the meaning of sacrifice in many religions. Its sacraments have been devalued because the Catholic insistence on trans-substantiation (the physical changing of bread and wine into Christ's body and blood) diminished the power of the metaphor.

It is instructive to catalogue some of God's less gentle characteristics in the Old and New Testaments to see just how closely in fact they dovetail with man's deep, and often dark, unconscious.

- He is 'a jealous God, visiting the sins of the fathers on their children to the third and fourth generation.' *(Exodus 20:5)* 'The Lord your God is a jealous God, a devouring fire.' *(Deut. 4:24)*
- At times He is an unforgiving God, especially if His people follow other gods. 'If you forsake the Lord and serve other Gods, then He will turn and do you harm, and consume you, after having done you good.' *(Joshua 24:20)*
- He is a God who can hate. 'I hate, I despise your feasts, and I take no delight in your solemn assemblies.' *(Amos 5:21)* 'The Lord God has sworn by himself "I abhor the pride of Jacob, and hate his strongholds, and I will deliver up the city and all that is in it."' *(Amos 6:8)*
- He is frequently intolerant, racist, an encourager of slavery, devious, harsh and judgemental. His views on sex are prescriptive, homophobic, requiring circumcision and so on.

Even in the New Testament, with Jesus's emphasis on love and forgiveness, there are examples of our harsher archetypes peeping through.

- If anyone comes to me and does not hate his own father and mother and wife and children, yes, and even his own life, he cannot be my disciple. *(Luke 14:26)*
- The master commended the unjust steward for his shrewdness; for the sons of this world are more

shrewd in dealing with their own generation than the sons of light. *(Luke 16:8)*

- The parable of the sheep and goats *(Matthew 25:31-46)* which condemns utterly those who have not been charitable in this life.

Indeed, it is arguable that the whole tenor of the New Testament is ultimately unforgiving, offering hell-fire to those condemned.

This is not in any sense to denigrate either Judaism or Christianity, but simply to observe that in reality both religions actually envisage a God who conforms more to the full panoply of our collective unconscious than our present-day susceptibilities imagine. We see it writ large in the other Abrahamic religion, Islam, at this stage of its evolution, and we are horrified at the brutality on display. We forget that we don't have to delve very far back in our own to discover just the same intolerance and savagery: and my point is that these savage instincts, along with a lot more noble ones, are part of our common heritage, our collective unconscious.

Jung's point in *Psychology and Religion* is that, this being so, organised religion should be offering rites, sacraments, confession and absolution along with ceremonial and crowd-savvy services which connect a congregation to its collective unknown knowns, not palming them off with a weak mix of love and forgiveness and the 'fatherly love' of God which he sees as a lie, a snare and a delusion. Rumbustious, pulpit-thumping, hell-fire preachers have gone out of fashion in our genteel established Church of England – and with them have gone most of the congregation. On the other hand in his Free Presbyterian Church of Ulster the Reverend Ian Paisley gained a huge following in Northern Ireland when, following the Anglo-Irish agreement of 1985 he called down the wrath of God on the head of Margaret Thatcher.

I'd like to end with a list of the very considerable advantages a religion based on the assumption that *'the God within'* inhabits our collective unconscious and is attainable by several means has to offer.

1) Firstly, this God can be reached in a service, in the company of others, for all our experience of crowds reinforces the truth that our collective unconscious comes to the fore in crowds, who take on a collective identity. A religious service should acknowledge and use this to good effect, strengthening common welfare, common purpose and a spirit of unity.

2) Secondly, this God within is eminently reachable individually too. Consulting the I Ching is like prayer, but prayer which is a conversation, where our unknowns become known, our deepest secrets, hidden even from ourselves, are laid bare to us, our waywardness acknowledged and understood, and our way forward clearly shown.

3) So many of the simpler Christian teachings become almost commonplace. Since the unconscious is collective, and shared by all, we all come with the same archetypes in our unconscious: archetypes which will blight us if we ignore them, and bless us if we seek them out. We do not need to posit a karma, a life hereafter when all wrongs will be righted, or a series of reincarnations where a 'soul' is increasingly purified. Each person carries his or her own mentor and scourge in their unconscious, and transgressions against it can be seen to damage that individual. Heaven and Hell are here and now, if you like.

4) The more complex dogmas and doctrines at least of the Christian church cease to perplex, if we recognise that they are projections of unconscious archetypes, not intended to be rationalised.

5) Jesus is seen as a man. He is a man supremely in touch with his unknown knowns, so much so that he is at one with them, and in that sense perhaps one might call him divine: but we don't need to invent a Trinity to understand his relationship with his God within.

6) We remove the difficult concept of a loving Father-God who nevertheless allows evil, early death, earthquakes, famine and flood. The God within is as capricious as our collective unconscious, sometimes

selfish, sometimes the trickster, sometimes the seductive anima, sometimes the universal mother, and so on. Importantly, though, this God is *within*. The external features of earth – flood, earthquake, volcanic eruptions – are not visited upon us by an external God.

Are we grown-up enough to be able to cope with such a religion? Could such an abstract concept command respect, attendance at common worship, and effort on a par with the church-building and welfare work of previous generations? Certainly it seems to be true that all religions so far have needed a charismatic figure or a panoply of gods with personalities in order to succeed. Or is it the case at least in the civilised West that we have outgrown all 'personified' religions?

To quote St Paul again: "When I was a child, I spoke like a child, I thought like a child, I reasoned like a child; when I became a man I gave up childish ways. For now we see through a glass darkly, but then face to face. Now I know in part; then I shall understand fully, even as I have been fully understood." *(1 Corinthians 13: 11,12)* That's a pretty good definition of our unknown knowns. Have we grown beyond childhood?

Chapter four

Accessing our Unknown Knowns

There are many ways of becoming aware of our unconscious, some deliberate activities, others more passively experienced. Music can raise the veil between consciousness and the unconscious – the more so when experienced collectively at either an orchestral concert or a rock festival. Likewise drama or ballet have the power to move us. Dancing ourselves, if we can move beyond embarrassment or conscious effort, can release us from the bonds of consciousness. Crowds of any sort move towards the collective unconscious, including of course congregations meeting specifically for worship. The word 'worship' itself means variously: to show profound religious devotion and respect to; adore or venerate; the formal expression of religious adoration *(Collins English Dictionary)*. Adoration generally takes us into archetype territory; it is a feeling deeper than the strictly conscious, often felt in the presence of our Anima/Animus, and it is observable how many times sex and religion coalesce.

On the personal scale there are also many ways of contacting the unconscious, which have been in use from pre-history. Asceticism has a long pedigree, appearing in all the world's religions. Hindus have their Sadhus, sometimes performing astonishing acts of sense-denial such as holding one arm aloft for years on end. Jainism, one of the oldest of the world's religions, also has one of the strictest of ascetic regimes for those who choose to follow with fasting, yoga practices, meditation in difficult postures, and other austerities. Judaism once practised asceticism, with the prophets in particular fasting to extremes and living as hermits, but modern day Judaism has largely eschewed the practice. The same is largely true of Christianity. In its early days ascetics such as Simeon Stylites took escape from the flesh to extremes: he lived for thirty seven years on a small platform atop a mast outside Aleppo in Syria. The idea of denying the senses lived on through the middle ages with anchorites and anchoresses living walled up in a cathedral's wall, with only a small window looking out on to the altar. Perhaps the most famous was Julian of Norwich. Other religions have honed different techniques, such as the whirling dances of the dervishes of Sufi Islam.

Less dramatic than asceticism, meditation also serves in virtually all religions as a means of moving out of the conscious plane and into that of the unconscious. Hinduism created Yoga as a physical and spiritual aid to escaping the conscious mind, while Buddhism developed the 'eightfold path', and its offspring, Zen, developed its unique form of meditation, the koan, a puzzle without an apparent answer, such as 'the sound of one hand clapping'. Judaism has given us the Qabalah, a symbolic code designed to further practitioner's spiritual development. Its central symbol is the Tree of Life, composed of eleven spheres interconnected by twenty two pathways. Christianity, at least in the Catholic tradition, has majored on 'telling the rosary', continually fingering rosary beads while repeating various mantras or prayers, such as the Hail Mary. Transcendental meditation burst on the world in the wake of the Beatles' visit to Maharishi Mahesh Yogi, and as its name implies it seeks to help a practitioner transcend consciousness to reach unconscious awareness.

All these techniques are valid, and all do help reveal our unknown knowns. But the one I want to recommend and explore fully is the I Ching, or Chinese Book of Changes. I have four good reasons for propounding this method of accessing our collective unconscious – or, if you prefer, communicating with the God within. The first is simply that I have found, over a thirty year period of usage, that it really does work. I ask a question or query a situation, and the I Ching generally gives me an answer to ponder and mull over, and finally to accept as valid. Secondly, Jung, originator of the collective unconscious thesis, was also an avid user for the last forty years of his life, and makes a strong case for its validity. Thirdly, consulting the I Ching is much less arduous than either meditation or asceticism. And lastly, and by far the most important, there is an astonishing and detailed connection between the format of the I Ching and the way our DNA makes the codons which create and sustain all forms of life.

It is generally the case that if several different phenomena can be demonstrated to follow an identical mathematical pattern then there is a fundamental connection between the phenomena. For instance, the Fibonacci Sequence – 0,1,1,2,3,5,8,13,21,34, 55,89,144… where each succeeding number is obtained by adding the two previous numbers, applies to many different aspects of nature. The leaf arrangement in plants, the pattern of the florets of a flower, the bracts of a pinecone, or the scales of a pineapple all follow the Fibonacci sequence of numbers. Sunflowers can get as far as the number 89, or even 144. Many other plants, such as succulents, also show the numbers. Some coniferous trees show these numbers in the bumps on their trunks. And palm trees show the numbers in the rings on their trunks. The sequence applies to natural phenomena as diverse as honey bees and the shell of the chambered Nautilus. And the ratio of succeeding pairs of numbers quickly converges to the number 1.618 – or it's inverse 0.618 – which is known as the Golden Ratio, classically the perfect ratio for beauty.

These connections are not arbitrary: they all stem from fundamental biological principles. In plants, having leaves or petals in a series approaching the golden ratio achieves the maximum amount of sunlight per petal, and so is an evolutionary development. In animals the golden ratio seems to be the norm as a proportion with regard to lengths of limbs – for instance the lengths of succeeding bones in fingers, forearm and hand, height to navel as a proportion of total height – all are roughly 1.618. This may well be because DNA molecules themselves follow this sequence, measuring 21 angstroms wide and 34 angstroms long for each full cycle of the double helix – successive Fibonacci numbers.

I will argue that the correspondence between the I Ching and DNA is also not coincidental, but signifies a deep connection between the two, justifying the use of the I Ching to access our deepest unknown knowns. It is time now to introduce the I Ching properly, including its pedigree, history, format and usage.

INTRODUCTION TO THE I CHING

The Chinese Book of Changes – The I Ching – is a collection of philosophical wisdom dating from about 3,000 BC, but codified and enhanced around 1,000 BC, and expanded, possibly by Confucius, around 500 BC. Richard Wilhelm, a close friend of Carl Jung, first published his German translation in 1923/4, to Jung's delighted, but private, approval. Cary F. Baynes was the widow of Helton Godwin Baynes, a friend and associate of Jung, and when she translated Wilhelm's German into English in 1949 Jung contributed a fulsome foreword some 19 pages long in which he acknowledges that he has used the I Ching for nearly thirty years as a means of exploring the unconscious. He also acknowledges his disquiet at being publicly associated, as an eminent psychotherapist now in his seventies, with a book of oracles which defy the Western concept of causality – cause and effect. He admits that this disquiet has prevented him from discussing the I Ching publicly until this moment. As he says himself, "It is a dubious task indeed to try to introduce to a critical modern public a collection of archaic 'magic spells', with the idea of making them more or less acceptable. I have undertaken it because I myself think there is more to the ancient Chinese way of thinking than meets the eye. But it is embarrassing to me that I must appeal to the good will and imagination of the reader, inasmuch as I have to take him into the obscurity of an age-old magic ritual." *(Foreword to Cary F. Baynes translation of Wilhelm's translation of the I Ching, p. xxxiii).*

I share his embarrassment, but three Twentieth Century discoveries make the journey both intellectually defensible and exciting. These are:

- The insights of Quantum Physics, and especially the concept of 'entanglement'. Oddly, given that Jung spent a lifetime developing his ideas on 'synchronicity' (his word for the fact that meaningfully related events often happen spontaneously at the same time), and his long-term friendship and collaboration with Wolfgang Pauli, one of Quantum Mechanics' chief exponents, Jung never appeals to quantum insights. We will try to address this in the section on synchronicity. (Chapter ten).
- The discovery in 1953 by Watson and Crick's team of DNA and its fundamental part in all living organisms.
- The realisation, in the 1990s, by Dr Martin Schönberger and later Katya Walter, that there is a direct mathematical correspondence between DNA and the pattern of the 64 I Ching hexagrams.

We will explore all three on our journey in this book.

Before we get embroiled in the complexities, though, we will first concentrate on the I Ching's philosophies and recommendations for living well. The Book of Changes covers 64 separate common human situations with down-to-earth practical advice for the best ways of conducting oneself, and in each case six possible ways in which the situation may change, of its own accord, or may be changed by the person caught up in the midst of it all. At first sight the readings seem quite prosaic and full of 'common sense'. It is only on deeper inquiry that one begins to recognise Jung's archetypes hidden within them. Much of their advice is on how to mitigate the power of an archetype to overwhelm and destroy. For the sake of an example's clarity, here's one of the situations along with the six likely changes that should be expected, in my paraphrase.

Enthusiasm (Number 16).

The essence of Enthusiasm is devotion within a movement. When a leader meets with a devoted response from people enthusiasm is bred, and the movement carries all before it. We can all think of movements that have attracted huge numbers of enthusiastic followers, sometimes with largely beneficial results, as in, for instance, the Quaker movement started by George Fry in the mid-Seventeenth Century. Others, such as the Nazi Party, following Adolf Hitler, have been an unmitigated disaster. The I Ching first describes the state of enthusiasm, then posits six ways it may progress and change into something different. The description of the state follows a template: firstly a description of 'THE CONDITION', secondly a comment on the condition – 'THE JUDGEMENT', and lastly a comment on the particular set of six lines which are held to describe the condition – 'THE IMAGE'. In the original Chinese these are short, pithy epigrams: Confucius (or whoever expanded the codex around 500 BC) expanded these, and translators have usually added their own comments to better illustrate the point for Western readers. James Legge, the first to translate into English, adds his own aids in parentheses, which preserves the 'original' text. Wilhelm, and hence Cary F. Baynes, is less punctilious in distinguishing the original from his more helpful expansions. In my renderings I will quote from his (translated) translation of the original Chinese in italics, with some of the expansions in plain font.

Each situation and reading is formed by combining two of the basic elements from the list of eight given in the previous chapter. The situation 'Enthusiasm' is formed by the combination of Earth (The Receptive) followed by Thunder (The Arousing).

THE CONDITION

Earth also has devotion as one of its attributes, and Thunder speaks of movement, something happening. The movement, along the line of least resistance, accords with the law of movement both in natural events and in human life. When these conditions apply, we may expect an enthusiastic response.

THE JUDGEMENT

> *It furthers one to install helpers.*
> *And to set armies marching.*

The time of enthusiasm derives from the fact that there is at hand an eminent man who is in sympathy with the spirit of the people and acts in accord with it.... To arouse enthusiasm it is necessary for a man to adjust himself and his ordinances to the character of those whom he has to lead..... It is enthusiasm that enables us to install helpers for the completion of an undertaking without fear of secret opposition. It is enthusiasm too that can unify mass movements, as in war, so that they can achieve victory.

THE IMAGE

Thunder comes resounding out of the earth:
The image of enthusiasm.
Thus the ancient kings made music
In order to honour merit,
And offered it with splendour
To the Supreme Deity,
Inviting their ancestors to be present.

As summer begins, thunder comes forth to refresh nature and to resolve tension.... So too, music in sacred ceremonies brings joy and relief in song and dance. And in solemn moments of religious inspiration it refreshes and sanctifies the people.... In these rites is manifest the mystical bond between God and man: the summation of culture. He who wholly comprehends this has, as it were, the world spinning in his hand.

THE SIX DEGREES OF CHANGE ASSOCIATED WITH 'ENTHUSIASM'.

1) Enthusiasm that boasts. A misfortune.

If we boast enthusiastically about our position, we invite misfortune. Enthusiasm is justified only when it is a general feeling that unites one with others, never as an egotistical emotion. Be cautious, reserved.

2) Be correct in a time of enthusiasm. Persevere in inner steadfastness.
To be ready to withdraw is prudent.

In other words, don't be dazzled by enthusiasm. Don't flatter the leaders, or neglect the followers. Recognise the signs of the times, and be ready to withdraw if there is discord. Remain self-reliant.

> 3) *Beware looking up to a leader, and beware also hesitating when it is time to act.*

Enthusiastic looking up to a leader shows weakness, dependence, lack of self-reliance. Being self-reliant, one must seize the moment if the time is right for action.

> 4) *A good leader gathers friends as hair is gathered in a clasp. Much is achieved.*

When someone is able to raise enthusiasm by their own sureness and freedom from hesitation they attract people because they have no doubts and are wholly sincere. Confidence in one's followers wins enthusiastic co-operation and hence success.

> 5) *Obstructed enthusiasm leads to frustration, but may bring salvation.*

Sometimes we find our enthusiasm obstructed, and it feels entirely negative. But in fact it may be preventing us from consuming all our energies in an empty, pointless enthusiasm.

> 6) *A deluded enthusiasm will not last for ever. To awaken from it is good.*

It is bad to let oneself be deluded by enthusiasm. But if the delusion has run its course and one can still change all is not lost. A sober awakening from a false enthusiasm is always possible, and is very favourable.

Many archetypes may show their faces in Enthusiasm, but perhaps the most obvious is that of 'the trickster'. Mob control seems his speciality, and a mob quickly loses conscious inhibition and fairness and behaves in an unpredictable, unsavoury trickster fashion. Football crowds have become more controlled, but at their worst display all the unpleasant, tribal, trickster elements of our collective unconscious. Inasmuch as the situation in I Ching terms is a mixture of the Thunder and the Earth motifs, as we will explore later, we should expect elements of the Animus and the Mother archetypes, and a moment or two's thought shows how they are involved in Enthusiasm. The leader of a movement is usually charismatic, and it is often the case that female followers can be seen to idealise him. The cause itself often offers a refuge, a club, a gang – a mother figure, in other words.

Let's put some flesh on the bones above by looking at a particular enthusiasm and seeing how the six changes above might assist us to act well.

Example: Religious cults.

Christianity throws up various cults and sects on a fairly regular basis. I want to look at the recurring phenomenon of Pentecostalism. The name comes from the account in The Acts of the Apostles, chapter 2, where the disciples, on the Day of Pentecost, after Jesus' crucifixion, are 'baptised in the Holy Spirit'. Additional material is taken from St. Paul's teaching, with particular reference to The First Letter to the Corinthians, chapter 12, where Paul enumerates various 'gifts of the Spirit' such as 'speaking in tongues', prophecy, healing powers, working miracles and so on.

Each time this raises its head it brings both renewal to the church and also great division. The enthusiasm that is generated by charismatic leaders claiming to be able to exercise these 'gifts of the Spirit' can be, and is, used for both good and ill. Taking the six change scenarios for Enthusiasm, let's see how much light each can throw on the situation.

1) Enthusiasm that boasts. A misfortune.
There is a definite tendency in each religious revival to set up an 'enlightened inner core' who see themselves as superior. Arguably even Jesus' original twelve disciples come into this category, and are sometimes chastised by Jesus for it *(e.g. Mark 9:34-37)*. This tendency always diminishes the legitimacy of the sect, and generally leads to its demise.

2) Be correct in a time of enthusiasm. Persevere in inner steadfastness. To be ready to withdraw is prudent.
In our example of Pentecostalism, this warning is to keep a clear perspective on the movement; to check that it is based on the whole Bible, not just on a few selected texts. If one sees imbalance, it is time to withdraw.

3) Beware looking up to a leader, and beware also hesitating when it is time to act.

Charismatic religious leaders are very prone to error. See for example so many of the American TV evangelists whose private lives let them down, or who descend into fraud and embezzlement. This warning is never to accord a leader uncritical respect, and always to speak up if it is clear they are wrong.

> 4) *A good leader gathers friends as hair is gathered in a clasp. Much is achieved.*

On the other hand there are honourable, balanced leaders who can genuinely bring much good to the church. In South Africa, Bishop Desmond Tutu, genuinely a Pentecostalist, is one such, whose ministry has contributed much to the generally peaceful transition to democratic rule.

> 5) *Obstructed enthusiasm leads to frustration, but may bring salvation.*

Very often hard-pressed vicars and priests have the difficult task of pointing out to enthusiastic church members following the latest 'new way' how unbalanced it may be. Frustration follows, but may aid some to see that their enthusiasm may be misplaced.

> 6) *A deluded enthusiasm will not last for ever. To awaken from it is good.*

Of all the new sects that have risen in the church over the centuries, only a few survive long. Protestant churches, breaking from the Roman church, have generally flourished, and among them off-shoots such as Quakers and Methodists have stood a fair test of time, but the more extreme, such as The Shakers have not. Inasmuch as their doctrines were too narrow, 'awakening from them' is good.

The treatment above is typical of the I Ching approach. Every situation we may find ourselves in has the potential to be beneficial or harmful, and the result is often decided by the way we conduct ourselves. It is good, therefore, to be aware of the probable results of differing actions and reactions in a situation, and the I Ching's 64 Situations, each with six likely changes, covers most of human life, and are well worthy of study.

THE BUILDING BLOCKS

The basic images

As observed in the preceding chapter, the I Ching philosophy is constructed from fundamental elements, which are metaphors for the various aspects of our personalities, and which combine to demonstrate the archetypes in our collective unconscious. There are eight elements in this, each with its own characteristics. Each element is given its image, its picture, and each conveys human attributes. For the sake of clarity, let's see them in tabular form.

Situation/characteristic	Attributes	Image or picture
THE CREATIVE	Strong, active	HEAVEN
THE RECEPTIVE	Devoted, yielding	EARTH
THE AROUSING	Inciting movement	THUNDER
THE ABYSMAL	Dangerous	WATER
KEEPING STILL	Resting, calm, firm, quiet	MOUNTAIN
THE GENTLE	Penetrating, enduring	WIND or WOOD
THE CLINGING	Light-giving, clarity	FIRE
THE JOYOUS	Joyousness	LAKE

These eight 'building blocks' are paired together in the Book of Changes, to give the 8 x 8 = 64 different readings, which are translated as situations such as 'Enthusiasm', 'The Receptive' and so on as we have seen. So, in ancient Chinese thought, Enthusiasm (No. 16) for example, is seen as the pairing of Thunder and the Earth, which is very different from the pairing of The Earth with Thunder, which gives Reading No. 24, 'The Turning Point'. This is far from obvious to Western eyes, which might assume symmetry in pairing, and so end up with only 32 readings.

Why should Thunder followed by Earth produce a reading about Enthusiasm? Looking at the attributes we see the incitement of movement followed by devotion and yielding: a pretty fair description of Enthusiasm and the sects it spawns. The other way round, though, a devoted, yielding group beginning to incite movement, and you can easily see we have a Turning Point, where something is about to happen. Clearly, there is no symmetry, and it is correct to assert that there are 64 distinct pairings, depending on which comes first.

To give another example, more or less at random, Mountain followed by Fire gives reading 22, Grace, or Adornment. In attribute terms, this is where something is at rest, still and calm, and then is given clarity, lightness. In other words the fundamental solid, still element is adorned, decorated, given an extra element of Grace. The other way round – Fire on a Mountain, gives reading 56: The Wanderer. In this case the image is of fire rushing across a mountain face, moving rapidly on: the image of a wanderer on the face of the earth, with no fixed abode.

This may all seem a bit fanciful to Western eyes, but it is really nothing more than the prolonged use of metaphor in describing what are very real human situations. The deeper reality behind the Chinese thought on this is that images, pictures and metaphors transcend racial divides, geographical boundaries and social norms to have the same meaning to all humanity. They are, indeed, the tools we use to reach into the unconscious, to dip down into the archetypes, and as such are the most appropriate describers of the situations we commonly find ourselves embroiled in.

SOME COMMON METAPHORS

As well as having its image, as shown above, each basic building block has various metaphorical allusions too, in terms of colour, associated animal, associated mineral and so on. These metaphors allow for a greater diversity in the interpretation of a particular pairing of building blocks than the straight-forward example in the previous chapter. Again, let's take a couple of examples before religiously tabling the full list of associated metaphors in the Chinese thought. You will recognise Jung's archetypes beginning to make their presence felt.

Here is part of the list for The Abysmal, whose image is Water:

The Abysmal is Water, ditches, ambush, bending and straightening out, bow and wheel. Among men it means the melancholy. It is associated with the fox.

The list for The Clinging, whose image is Fire, is as follows:

The Clinging is fire, the sun, lightning, the middle daughter. It means coats of mail and helmets; lances and weapons. Among men it means the big-bellied. It is the sign of dryness: it symbolises the tortoise, the crab, the snail, the mussel, the hawkbill tortoise. Among trees it means those that dry out in the upper part of the trunk.

Without worrying, for now, why these symbols should come to be associated with their particular building block, let's see how they are used in the two readings built from these blocks: Fire above Water and Water above Fire.

The first is No 64, Transition (before completion).

Transition (before completion). No. 64

Within the judgement on this (fairly common) human condition we find the following metaphor.

The caution of a fox walking over ice is proverbial in China. His ears are constantly alert to the cracking of the ice as he carefully and circumspectly searches out the safest spots. But a young fox who has not yet acquired this caution goes ahead boldly, so he falls in and gets his tail wet. Even though he is almost across the water, his efforts will still have been in vain. Accordingly, in times before completion, during transition, deliberation and caution are the prerequisites of success.

The first degree of change repeats this metaphor:

1) One gets one's tail wet. Humiliation.

In times of disorder there is the temptation to advance as rapidly as possible to get results. But if the time is not yet right this enthusiasm

59

leads only to failure. One's tail gets wet because one cannot take the end into view: one is too rash. It is better to spare oneself and hold back.

Water above Fire moves us on to the state of Order (after completion).

Order (after completion). No 63

The image for this is that of a kettle hanging over a fire. Preparations are complete and we may look forward to tea! However, the relationship always needs care, for if the water boils over the fire will be put out and the energy lost; likewise, if the fire is too hot the water will boil off and be lost.

In life, too, there are times when all the forces are in balance, working in harmony, and all seems in the best of order. Then, only the sage recognises the moments that bode danger and knows how to avoid it.

Both readings clearly invoke the archetype of the 'wise old man' – the sage – who knows that 'there's many a slip 'twixt cup and lip'. In both these cases there is an element of metaphor used in order to bring out the full meaning of the two states, and this is very often true in the various combinations of the 'building blocks', and in the six degrees of change accompanying each.

HOW ARE THE BUILDING BLOCKS CONSTRUCTED?

Ancient Chinese thought sees human reality in terms of the principles of yin and yang. Yin and yang are specific Chinese constructs, but they have their counterparts in every culture, for what they describe are fundamental elements in all human societies. Yin is the image for a whole range of prototypes: mother, earth, Mother Earth, darkness, cold, yielding, acceptance, passivity. Yang is the image for the opposite types: father, heaven, light, heat, forcefulness, creativity, activity. One of the basic premises of the I Ching is to recognise that any situation may appear to be wholly of a yin type – for instance motherhood – and yet will contain within it the seed of a yang type. (Motherhood for instance is supremely creative). In the same way conditions that seem purely yang, aggression say, contain a seed of a yin characteristic – perhaps a frustrated need to be loved.

The concept of yin and yang has its own symbol, shown above, now quite common in Western literature. Its Chinese name is the Taijitu but it's more commonly called the Yin-Yang symbol or the Tai Chi. Here the left hand dark area represents yin, but note that it has a light dot of yang embedded in it. The right hand light area represents yang, but has a dot of darkness embedded in it too. This symbolism is fundamental to I Ching: any situation, any characteristic, has the seeds of its opposite inherently within it. Change is inescapable!

Think of any characteristic you may have – let's take arrogance, a certainty that you are always right and others who disagree therefore wrong. Of itself this is a very yang characteristic, male, strong, dominating. Scratch a little deeper and you will find arrogance often masks a fear of inadequacy, probably unacknowledged – a very yin characteristic. Taoism, the Chinese philosophy from which the I Ching comes, is built on the understanding that every human trait, and every situation, contains within it the seeds of its opposite. You can do this with any trait you care to pick: pride/modesty; anger/passivity; selfishness/caring etc. A moment or two's thought shows that each does indeed carry the seed of its opposite.

Yin and yang each have their own symbol or hieroglyph. Yin is represented by a broken line ▬ ▬ and yang by an unbroken line ▬▬▬ . The only reason I've been able to unearth for this is somewhat esoteric: the story that long ago lines were scratched on a (dead) tortoise shell, the shell heated then dunked in water so it cracked, and any scratch broken by a crack was interpreted as a 'no', yin; any scratch not broken by a crack was a 'yes', yang. Whatever the truth, the symbols are deeply embedded in the I Ching to the extent that sometimes an image is made by the juxtaposition of broken and unbroken lines producing a picture – e.g. an open mouth.

This was the earliest, and most primitive, idea of divination, with the only possible answers being yes, yang, or no, yin. Very like our tossing of a coin to make a decision! Early on in the Chinese annals of divination there was felt the need for a bit more subtlety and two answers were sought, which could be yin and yin; yin and yang; yang and yin; or yang and yang. These were represented by two lines, respectively for the above ▬ ▬; ▬ ▬; ▬▬; ▬▬ . Note here the first oddity to Western eyes. **The Chinese start from the bottom up, so yin followed by yang has yin on the bottom. This is always the case.** Presumably ▬ ▬ meant a definite no, ▬ ▬ sort of probably no, or no changing to yes, and so on. These were codified as, respectively, fixed yin; moving yin; moving yang; and fixed yang. Here we see the fundamental concept of Change first introduced.

Coincidentally, this is the same pattern Donald Rumsfeld came up with in our introduction. 'Known knowns' – they would be ▬▬, fixed, definite yang. 'Known unknowns' would be ▬ ▬, moving yin, an unknown on its way to being known. 'Unknown unknowns' of course are ▬ ▬, definitely unknown, fixed yin. And the one he didn't mention, 'Unknown knowns' must be ▬▬, things we should know, but which are well on the way to being unknown, moving yang.

A little later in the process someone decided to put three lines together. This might have been no more than the old trick of 'best out of three' when the first toss of a coin doesn't give us the answer we wanted. Three lines arrayed like this are called a Trigram, and there are eight of them, from yang yang yang right though to yin yin yin. Symbolically the eight trigrams are

Reading from the **bottom upwards** as always in the I Ching these give, from left to right, yang yang yang; yang yang yin; yang yin yang; yin yang yang; yang yin yin; yin yang yin; yin yin yang; and yin yin yin.

This development started this whole branch of philosophy, with various interpretations being put on the eight trigrams, so that whichever your three coin tossing produced various conclusions could be drawn. Of course back in early China it wasn't coin tossing, but the actual mechanism needn't concern us yet. What does need to concern us are the interpretations they put on each trigram. These interpretations were the building blocks we introduced at the beginning of the chapter, and reading from the left the trigrams above represent:

Heaven; Lake; Fire; Wood/ Wind; Thunder; Water; Mountain; Earth

As we also saw, the next development, way back in the China of 3 - 5,000 years ago, was to combine two building blocks together, so generating the 64 possible readings. This gives what is known in the literature as 'Hexagrams', that is blocks of six lines of Yang and Yin combined, drawn as, for instance,

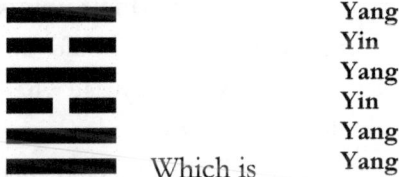

	Yang
	Yin
	Yang
	Yin
	Yang
Which is	**Yang**

Remembering that we read from the bottom upwards this is Yang, yang, yin, yang, yin, yang. In terms of our basic building blocks, the trigrams, it is Fire above Lake, which gives Reading No. 38: Opposition. If we had been generating it by simply tossing a coin, it would have been head, head, tail, head, tail, head, as we build from the bottom upwards.

I have split this reading, as indeed all the readings, into three sections: **THE CONDITION,** which describes the situation being pictured; **THE JUDGEMENT** where the I Ching goes through the various archetypes that might be in our unconscious at this time; and **THE IMAGE**, generally two to four lines on an idea generated by the hexagram, or rather, the juxtaposition of the two trigrams that make it up. Our convention is that lines which are a direct translation of the Chinese are in italics; my amplification in normal font. In this case, we have:

Reading No. 38, Opposition
THE CONDITION

Fire and water (in the lake) are by nature opposed. Fire evaporates water and so causes it to disappear: water will douse fire, and cause it to disappear, too. Oddly, the original Chinese apparently doesn't refer to this opposition, but to the fact that fire burns upwards, while water in the lake seeps downwards, and indeed the lake itself is as far down as it can get. The two movements are opposed, giving the idea of opposition, estrangement, misunderstanding. Hence this hexagram (number 38) is entitled 'Opposition'.

THE JUDGEMENT

Opposition: in small matters, good fortune.

When people live in opposition and estrangement they cannot carry out a great undertaking in common; their points of view diverge too widely. In such circumstances one should above all not proceed brusquely, for that would only increase the existing opposition. Instead, one should limit oneself to producing gradual effects in small matters. Here success can still be expected, because the situation is such that the opposition does not preclude all agreement.

In general, opposition appears as an obstruction, but when it represents polarity within a comprehensive whole, it has also its useful and important functions. The oppositions of heaven and earth, spirit and nature, man and woman, when reconciled, bring about the creation and reproduction of life. In the world of visible things, the principle of opposites makes possible the differentiation by categories through which order is brought into the world.

THE IMAGE

Above fire; below, the lake:
The image of opposition.
Thus, amid all fellowship
The superior man retains his individuality.

The two elements, fire and water, never mingle but even when in contact retain their own natures. So the cultured man is never led into baseness or vulgarity through intercourse or community of interests with persons of another sort; regardless of all commingling he will always preserve his individuality.

If we tossed coins and generated this reading, and found it did indeed chime with a situation we found ourselves in, might reading through these three elements help us choose a path through the morass? Let's root it in a possible scenario. Say you are a mother with children in a primary school. You and your husband feel strongly that children should be allowed freedom and the chance to discover things for themselves, but the school's policy is to give a lot of homework, to be very prescriptive about lessons, and to concentrate on academic success rather than individual flowering. You consult the I Ching and generate this reading: how might it help you?

THE CONDITION you will recognise, but it will remind you that the different approaches are indeed very different and may perhaps be irreconcilable.

THE JUDGEMENT nevertheless cautions that you do try to bring some element of playfulness into the school day. Remember not to 'proceed brusquely' or you will merely put the teachers' backs up. Perhaps you can volunteer to take the children on nature walks? Or perhaps you have to say you cannot affect what goes on in school, but will make sure your own children at least will get the chance to discover for themselves at home, and will take them on journeys of exploration yourself. But the judgement is very much that you should not expect to change the whole tenor of the school's philosophy.

THE IMAGE If you are to be true to yourself it may even be that you have to find a different school for your children. You must 'retain your individuality'.

WHAT HAPPENED TO THE SIX DEGREES OF CHANGE?

You will remember that in chapter four each reading came with six associated 'degrees of change' which described how the situation might change of its own accord, or how we might seek to change it ourselves. In the example above, no such degrees of change have appeared, and it is not clear how they could be generated by the simple coin tossing mentioned. However, you may have put two and two together and thought to yourself "Ha, six degrees of change, and six lines in each hexagram. I wonder if they are connected?" They are: the first degree of change is associated with the first (bottom, remember) line of the hexagram, and so on. The connection harks back to the idea on page 62 of 'definite no' versus 'sort of no' – 'no changing to yes'. You will remember they were portrayed as ▬ ▬ and ▬▬▬, and generated by tossing a coin twice. Tail followed by tail was 'definite no' whereas tail followed by head was kind of 'no, but maybe changeable'.

This idea of a wobbly No, or a wobbly Yes, was introduced very early on into the I Ching. In those days they didn't toss coins, but had a much more esoteric system involving yarrow sticks, (see chapter nine), but for the sake of simplicity let's stick to the usual Western approach of coin tossing. How can we use a coin to make each line either definite or change-able? This is complicated by the need to make the probability of a 'definite yes' or a 'definite no' much more likely than a change-able yes or no, because that's how it was with the yarrow sticks. This makes what you might think is the natural answer – toss two coins – not appropriate, because a definite

No ⚏ ⚏ (Tail followed by tail) is just as likely as a changeable no ⚎ (Tail followed by head).

It turns out that tossing three coins to generate each line of the hexagram in practice gives almost exactly the 'right' likelihood of a No, a Yes, a changeable No and a changeable Yes as compared to the ancient Yarrow Stick method, so that is how the Western world generally goes about it. The three coins can come down in the following eight orders:

HHH, HHT, HTH, HTT, THH, THT, TTH, TTT

And each is equally likely. The convention is as follows:
One Head and two tails (in any order) is read as Yang.
One Tail and two Heads (in any order) is read as Yin.
All three Heads is read as changeable (or moving) Yang, and that line has generated one of the degrees of change.
All three Tails is read as changeable (or moving) Yin and that line has generated one of the degrees of change.

Let's ground this in a concrete example. Suppose your six separate throws of three coins each time produces the following results.

HHT, TTT, HTH, THT, THH, HHH

Stacking these up to make a hexagram, remembering to start at the bottom, we get

HHH		Moving Yang
THH	Which equates to	Yin
THT		Yang
HTH		Yin
TTT		Moving Yin
HHT		Yin

As yet we have symbols for Yang (━━━) and for Yin (━ ━) but no single symbol for moving (changeable) Yang or for moving Yin. The conventions for these new symbols are that moving Yang is written as ━⊖━ and moving Yin is written as ━✕━ .With this convention we can now construct our hexagram as

67

Now we can say we have generated, by tossing three coins six times over, the hexagram for Reading No. 38: Opposition, with the second and sixth degrees of change. Now, in addition to the Condition, Judgement and Image we had above, we are also directed to the 2nd (from the bottom, remember) and 6th degrees of change. These read, for Opposition:

  2) *One meets his Lord in a narrow street.*
An accidental meeting under informal circumstances may serve to bring together people estranged by a misunderstanding, provided they have an inner affinity. No blame attaches to such a meeting – you have not lost your way or given up your individuality.

  6) *One sees one's friends as sly. Danger. But then tension goes and*
      union comes.
Sometimes we get so isolated and estranged from those around that we misjudge even our best friends, and become defensive. We need to recognise our mistake and that they are in fact well-wishing; then the tension will be resolved in union and all will go well. Just when opposition reaches its climax it changes over to its antithesis.

In terms of our example, you might read these degrees of change as implying that there are actually many other parents on the same wavelength, and that if you come across one you should join forces in the fight.

Are you bristling at the very thought of taking any notice of such an arcane procedure? Does it seem almost insolent of me (or the I Ching) to provide advice? Remember what the I Ching claims; a very personal claim – that it will put you in touch with your own unconscious. No-one else is offering advice, you are bringing your own powers to bear on the problem, powers buried beneath rational thought in that cornucopia that is your own unconscious.

In principle you now have the bare bones of the I Ching at your fingertips, and you don't need any more understanding before going off and buying a book of the readings, or, in our internet age, going online and subscribing to one of the many websites providing readings. Why not give it a try? But remember, there is only one sort of question that the I Ching claims to be able to answer, and it's not 'Who's going to win the Grand National?' or even 'Will that girl/boy want to go out with me?' or even the more general 'What does the future hold for me?' No, the only sort of question it can throw any light on is the sort where you already know the answer… but it's buried deep in your unconscious. The answer is an archetype, or set of archetypes that you need to recognise are involved in the situation. Suitable questions then are such as 'Why am I finding it so difficult to do this job/like this person/get my own way/understand this person's point of view? Questions to do with situations and how you should react. Questions about relationships, about your attitude to money/possessions/positions of responsibility. These are vital questions, and you may be surprised at some of the answers… but those are the very answers you need at the time. They are your own unknown knowns.

You may well find it impossible to credit the oracular nature of the I Ching: after all, it defies all Western ideas of cause and effect for the mere spinning of coins to produce the one particular reading out of sixty-four which is appropriate to the situation you find yourself in. Jung also felt this impossibility keenly, and developed his theory of 'Synchronicity' (his word) to try to produce an argument that Westerners might accept. I have not included it here because I felt it disrupted the flow of the concept I am developing, but I have included his argument, and the possible impact of Quantum Mechanics on the argument, as chapters ten and eleven.

Chapter five

The metaphors

METAPHOR AND THE UNCONSCIOUS

It is a well-known phenomenon that many dreams are archetypal. That is to say, people the world over have the same sort of dreams in the same sort of situations. The dreams are metaphors for the situations – and they are universal. Let's look at a few classic examples, bearing in mind that we are amateurs, not psychologists!

> 1) *Failure to catch a bus/boat/aeroplane. A continual frustration in your attempts to do some (often simple) task. Alternatively, being in an exam you can't complete partly from lack of preparation, partly because the physical things (desk/pen/paper/time) conspire against you.*

This is a classic anxiety dream. If you are having dreams of this sort you can bet that in waking life there are situations where you feel stretched beyond your capabilities, either in terms of abilities, time constraints, other people's expectations, or even your own unrealistically high standards.

An I Ching reading that would be appropriate is No. 28, Great heaviness, where the metaphor is of a huge beam, sagging under its own weight, unable to bear the load put upon it.

> 2) *Dreams about falling. No matter where you are falling from, the metaphor is the very action of falling without any means of halting your fall. You are powerless to control the fall, but you know it will end in disaster.*

Again, this is partly an anxiety dream, but often in this case anxiety about an action you are going to take which your unconscious knows is foolish and will end badly. You are breaking society's taboos, and will be shamed. Mishandling money, cheating, having affairs, lying –

all are likely to provoke dreams of falling. Your unconscious is warning you of danger.

An example in the I Ching is No. 44, Encountering (coming to meet). The metaphor is that of a bold girl lightly surrendering herself and gaining power. The Judgement is all about how we should not imagine we can dally with things/people who seem harmless, for it will turn out badly. The falling dream warns of the same inevitable consequence.

3) Flying dreams. These come in two types: those where we feel gloriously in control and are swooping and travelling with ease; and those where we are finding it difficult to maintain being air-borne. Flying dreams are often 'lucid', that is, we are aware we are dreaming, and close to waking up. Indeed, we may almost consciously try to prolong the dream, as it is enjoyable.

These are the opposite of 'falling dreams': here we feel in control of our situation, 'on top of things'. But as usual, the balance is delicate, and the dream can easily turn into nightmare.

The I Ching has several examples using this metaphor. No. 62, for instance, is entitled 'Great Smallness' and the condition speaks of a soaring bird, but warns that it should not try to surpass itself and fly to the sun, but descend to earth, where its nest is.

4) Dreams about being naked.

These come in various guises, and indicate different things about our unconscious, depending on which type they are. Those where we are embarrassed about being naked in inappropriate situations tend to mean we have something to hide in real life, something we are ashamed of, but not ready to admit to. Alternatively, those where we alone are naked, in a crowd or with others we know, but are not embarrassed, indeed are proud of our nakedness, hint at a personality very much at ease with itself. Thirdly, dreaming about suddenly finding yourself naked in a work situation may well be your unconscious noting that you are ill-prepared for the job you are doing.

The I Ching has corresponding situations for all three of the above types. The first, where we are embarrassed, with something to hide, is covered in No. 18, Removing corruption. The Chinese character for this hexagram represents a bowl in whose contents worms and maggots are breeding – a common variant of the naked dream. The judgement affirms the need to discover what it is that our conscious mind is hiding before we can begin to remove the corruption in our spiritual lives. Take the 4th degree of change, for instance:

4) Tolerating decay leads to humiliation.

If we are too weak to take measures against decay, rooted in the past but now beginning to manifest itself, then it will run its course and humiliation will result. We gain nothing by letting things drift.

The second type of 'Naked dream', where we are proud of standing out in a crowd, is shown in reading No. 14, 'Possession in great measure.' It indicates a man of great inner wealth, in a position of authority, who is nevertheless unselfish, modest and kind. Unusually, all the degrees of change promise success, as long as the possessor of this greatness remains modest and unassuming, and does not let arrogance gain a foothold. Take the 5th degree of change, for instance:

5) He who makes his truth accessible, and yet remains dignified is favoured indeed.

People are won over by unaffected sincerity, not by coercion. (Surely the meaning of being unashamedly naked in a crowd?) But benevolence alone, in making your truth accessible, may lead to insolence. Such familiarity must be kept in bounds by dignity. As ever, being naked in a crowd walks a fine line between accessibility and lack of dignity!

And finally, the third type of Naked dream, suddenly realising that you, as emperor, have no clothes, betrays a unconscious recognition that you have been promoted beyond your capabilities, and are struggling to keep on top of things. Reading No. 33, Retreat (Withdrawal) recognises this situation and suggests the way out.

THE JUDGEMENT reads:

Seek success only in small matters. Persevere thus, in accord with the time.

Success lies in being able to retreat at the right time and in the right way. We must not miss the right moment for retreat while we are still in possession of power and position.

PAULI'S DREAMS.

The reason Jung gave for his surprising decision not to accept Wolfgang Pauli as a patient when he came to him in extremis in 1932 is as follows. 'He was chock-full of archaic material, and I said to myself: "Now I am going to make an interesting experiment to get that material absolutely pure, without any influence from myself, and therefore I won't touch it."' He referred Pauli to Dr. Erna Rosenbaum, "who was then just a beginner.... I was absolutely sure she would not tamper." *(The Tavistock Lectures: On the theory and practice of analytical psychology, 1968. Para 402)* This seems to show a rather chauvinistic disregard for Pauli's grave psychological state at the time, and for Rosenbaum's professionalism, but in practice it paid dividends over the next twenty-six years as Jung and Pauli met as friends, corresponded frequently, and tackled the question of an observer's unconscious (and conscious) mind affecting, and being affected by, experiments he might conduct. Pauli, as Jung recognised in their first meeting, was capable of reaching his own 'unknown knowns', his collective archetypes, with minimal professional input, and his state of mind improved significantly with Rosenbaum's professional and Jung's friendly ministrations.

Pauli's chief implement in accessing his unconscious was his dreams, and he had, and recorded, a prodigious number of them. He wrote to, and spoke with Jung about over thirteen hundred different dreams, and with his help used them both in his work as an innovative thinker in Quantum Mechanics and to sort out his desperately one-sided personality. The following are just a selection, demonstrating the fertile cross-pollination between the two experts in their increasingly complementary fields. In all cases references are to letters as translated in *Atom and Archetype: The Pauli/Jung letters 1932 – 1958,* edited by C A Meier.

Letters 13 -16.

Pauli describes a dream which is largely in terms of symbols from his field of study – as indeed most of his dreams are. As he commented himself: 'Others research physics; I dream physics.' In brief, his dream covers the idea of a magnetic field in which many small magnets align. Suddenly one magnet starts to rotate. This image is reinforced by one in which radioactive isotopes spontaneously begin to separate, and then by another in which the splitting of spectral lines is enhanced by a magnetic field into the 'fine structure' whereby each line is further differentiated. The dream then moves on to the radioactive nucleus of an isotope, and finally to the concept of 'resonance', where vibrations coincide with sometimes catastrophic consequences such as bridges being torn apart by oscillations caused by the wind.

Pauli gets well down the road of interpreting this dream for himself, and his conclusions are expanded and given psychological legitimacy by Jung. The magnetic field is seen as 'Heaven' in which the multiplicity of individual magnets are all the people in the world: their alignment both demonstrates their lack of individuality and their place in the self-regulating system of society. The rotating magnet is the beginning of the process of 'individuation' – melding conscious and unconscious. The isotopes and spectral lines reinforce the same idea of consciousness arising from the collective unconscious. Jung goes on to posit his fundamental principle of the collective unconscious: that it exists outside time and space. That is to say it applies to all mankind, everywhere, and throughout all time. He gives the example of a termite colony 'possessing only unconscious performing organs, whereas the centre, to which all the parts are related, is indivisible and not empirically demonstrable.'

He sees the radioactive nucleus as 'an excellent symbol for the source of energy of the collective unconscious, the ultimate external stratum of which appears as individual consciousness.' In other words the collective unconscious acts like the nucleus and inner spheres of an atom, providing all the energy needed to fire off an electron from the outer sphere – consciousness. In the same way the sun is the source of all the energy that is emanated as heat and light, which has always been pictured as rays coming from it. Here, at the beginning of their correspondence, we see the over-arching role of the collective unconscious, some of its archetypes, and the prospect of a marrying of the insights of physics and psychology.

Pauli replies (letter 16) in grateful terms, but draws attention to two lines in additional material he has sent Jung, in which the seven and the ace of clubs appear. He sees archetypes in both these: "In my seventh year my sister was born. *So the 7 is an indication of the birth of the anima.*" (His italics). "I can offer further evidence of the connection for me between the anima and number 7. In a much later dream the card with the 7 of diamonds came up, and it looked like this:

```
    X           X

    X       X   X

    X           X
```

"And then the 'Wise Man' in my dream explained to me that this also meant M and referred to Mother and to Mary." (Fortunately both beginning with M in German too).

Here Pauli is noting for himself the presence of three archetypes: the 'wise man', the mother and the anima. He goes on to discuss the anima in his dreams, who frequently appears as a Chinese woman, or sometimes as a 'dark lady'.

The ace of clubs Jung had described as being the shape of the cross, and therefore a religious archetype. Pauli rejects this interpretation and says that for him the ace of clubs is an archetype of Power, which returns in later dreams associated with 'the duke who chases the maid', further evidence of his search for his anima.

In fact Pauli's approach to women had always been infantile, as shown by his sordid exploits in the brothels of Hamburg, his short-lived first marriage to Käthe Margarethe Deppner, and his state of utter depression when he first came to Jung. He was typical of the genius scientist or mathematician, an excellent and intuitive thinker who had entirely neglected the feeling side of his nature and so was completely at sea in female company and not much better with men. The unknown known that he needed, above all, to access was his anima, his female side, and his dreams slowly led him on this crucial voyage of inward discovery. We look at a couple of the most seminal.

The veiled woman.

We are not told of the details of this dream, simply that it is the first time a woman has actually figured in one of Pauli's dreams. It is Jung who recognises her as his anima – his feminine side – and her veil as pertaining to an initiation rite: in this case Pauli's initiation into a more adult relationship with women. Together they recognise that Pauli's earlier projection of his anima, as is most men's, was on to his mother. She committed suicide by poisoning in reaction to Pauli's father's infidelities in 1927 – the beginning of Pauli's descent into depravity.

Pauli's mother.

A little while later Pauli dreamt of his mother pouring water from one basin to another, which he recognises as belonging to his sister Hertha. He realises he has transferred his anima projection from his dead mother to his sister, and confesses to Jung that any women he has fallen in love with either look like Hertha, or are her friends. Jung is upbeat about it all, and predicts (accurately, it turns out) that his anima will soon transfer to the unknown woman in his unconscious, still represented by the dark lady.

The sun worshipper.

It is not long before Pauli dreams that an unknown woman is standing on a globe, worshipping the sun. Jung claims her as Pauli's burgeoning anima, emerging from the ancient world he had condemned her to by his concentration on rationality over feeling. Pauli's mental state improves notably, and soon after these interchanges he meets and marries his second wife, Franziska Bertram, in 1934.

We could spend a long time on Pauli's dreams, but that taster is sufficient to show how he and Jung discovered various archetypes in them, and how the discovery itself was enough to open up Pauli's unknown knowns and help him to become a more rounded and grounded character than he was previously. We will return to these two giants after we have looked at DNA and its part in the story of the I Ching. By the time Watson and Crick and their team had made their world-changing discovery in 1953 Jung was 78 and Pauli a mere five years from his early death. There is no evidence that either studied the new knowledge but it is fascinating to ponder what they might have made of it in the light of their quest for unification between physics and psychology. We will return after we have established the intimate correspondence between the structures of the I Ching and DNA.

Just as our dreams use archetypal images, so the ancient Chinese philosophers worked on the earlier versions of the I Ching to bring metaphor into play to reinforce the readings they found there. Arguably this was carried to too great a length, building a fantastical edifice out of the basic building blocks, but the original intention, to provide insights into our unconscious minds, was sound enough. The result is a wealth of metaphor and image suffusing the readings and the degrees of change that allow each enquirer to choose that which has the greatest meaning to himself, and so to learn some inner truth from the reading.

CONFUCIUS AND THE TEN WINGS.

Richard Wilhelm introduces a discussion on the images and metaphors used throughout the I Ching with the claim that it was

Confucius himself, or at least his circle of disciples, who wrote down and developed the concepts, in a series of commentaries known as the Ten Wings, some five hundred years BC. Most important of these seems to be the Eighth Wing, in which Confucius propounds a series of metaphors and images for the eight basic 'building blocks', the Trigrams. These are important for the same reason as archetypal dreams: they open a door into the unconscious that just isn't possible using rational means. The images that generations of Chinese came up with are fundamental to all people as common metaphors of various unconscious states of mind.

The first of these pairs off the trigrams and their associated images in the following way.

"Heaven and earth determine the direction. The forces of mountain and lake are united. Thunder and wind arouse each other. Water and fire do not combat each other. Thus are the eight trigrams intermingled." This pairing is very ancient and is called the Sequence of Earlier Heaven, or the Primal Arrangement.

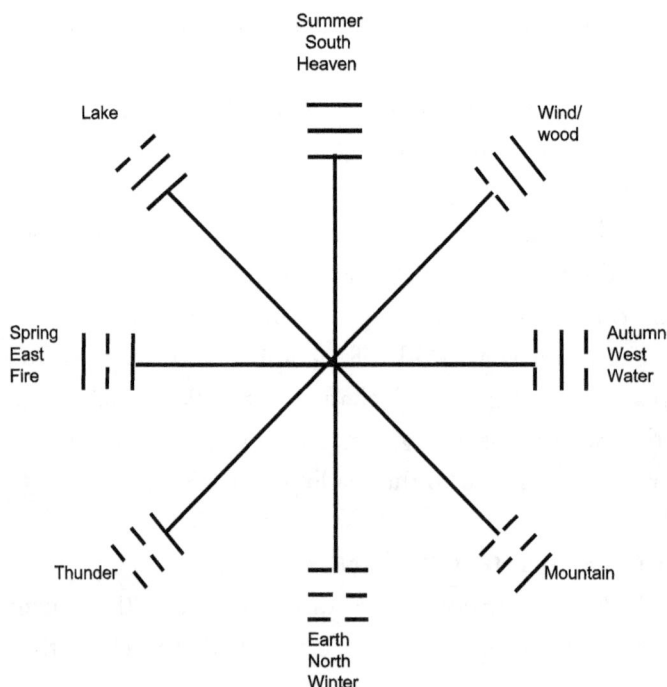

It is shown pictorially as a 'compass' with the eight trigrams on the eight primary points of the compass. As ever, the Chinese do things upside down from the Western way, so that South is at the top, East to the left, West to the right, and North at the bottom!

At first sight, to Western eyes, this seems completely random and incomprehensible, and of no help at all. The point behind the picture is to imagine going round the circle, clockwise, which gives the metaphor of the unfolding year, as we start (at the bottom, naturally!) with the Earth, then Thunder is seen as awakening the forces of nature, which, moving on to Fire in the East, giving warmth, causes nature to blossom and bloom. This brings Joy to mankind, symbolised by Lake, as we move on to Summer, and the creative, as all fruits are created. Then we move on to the winds of early autumn, as the new growth hardens into solid wood, and thence to autumn itself when the rains come with water, and finally to Mountain – Keeping Still, where nature takes a rest and creatures hibernate.

This may seem very arbitrary, but it has an important corollary: you can go backwards round the circle and demonstrate how life is compacted into a seed, and grows from that seed. Starting again at Earth, in the cold North (Bottom) and turning anti-clockwise, at first with Mountain we keep still: the seed, resting until Water is added, the next element, starting the irreversible growth. This growth produces (in plants) Wood, fibre, the stuff of life. Creation is at work, leading on to Joy (symbolised by Lake). The new life has energy, symbolised by Fire, and all the more so by the last in the reverse circle, Thunder.

The germ of this idea is that the trigrams do truly symbolise fundamental concepts, and are therefore natural to our unconscious. As the riddle used to go: 'Earth, water, fire and air; met together in a garden fair' with the answer 'Man'. So we recognise our constituents, our fundamental particles. As for the others, Thunder and Wind symbolise life-giving energy, Mountain and Lake the very earth we inhabit, our place.

The Chinese sages went on to describe this circle as a family, with a father, a mother, three daughters and three sons. This built up another layer of metaphor, to trigger more reactions in our unconscious, which, let us never lose sight, is the point behind all this symbolism. The order they chose for this 'Old Family' is highly instructive. Starting with Earth Mother ☷ they then went anti-clockwise round the 'compass' above, with Mountain, ☶ as 1st daughter; Water, ☵ as 2nd daughter; Wood/wind, ☴ as 3rd daughter…. Then clockwise up the East side for the sons, Thunder ☳ as 1st son; Fire, ☲ as 2nd son; Lake, ☱ as 3rd son; and finally Heaven, ☰, as father. In doing this they, wittingly or unwittingly, invented the binary number scale 4,500 years before Leibnitz had the idea in the Western world! Take ▬ ▬ as representing 0, zero, and ▬▬▬ as 1. The top line (last written) represents units; the middle line 2s and the bottom line 2 squared (= 4s).

☷ is the 0, zero; ☶ is one unit, no 2s and no 4s =1; ☵ is no units, one 2 and no 4s = 2; ☴ is one unit, one 2 and no 4s = 3; ☳ is no units, no 2s and one 4 = 4; ☲ is one unit, no 2s and one 4 = 5; ☱ is no units, one 2 and one 4 = 6; and ☰ is one unit, one 2 and one 4 = 7. It is this simple yet profound 'Old Family' arrangement that is the key to the astonishing correspondence with DNA that we will investigate in chapter seven.

Is there any point in this idea of 'the family?' They turn out to be archetypal unconscious images, having recognisable metaphorical allusions that we can in fact resonate with, and as such some of the judgements, and many of the changes, rely on the various images of sons and daughters. Confusingly, however, by the time the Confucian circle came to codify the metaphors the Family members had changed their spots to become 'The New Family', in which Father remains as Heaven ☰, Earth as Mother ☷, and Thunder as first son ☳; but middle son is now Water ☵, youngest son is Mountain ☶, eldest daughter is Wood/wind ☴, middle daughter is Fire ☲, and youngest daughter is Lake ☱. This was a logical development: all the sons have just one yang line, and the daughters just one yin. Eldest has the line at the bottom (first written), second on the second line and youngest on the third, top line. All the readings are based on this 'New Family'.

Let's take, as an example, Reading No. 17: Following.

READING No. 17: FOLLOWING

The upper trigram is Lake – family member 'the youngest daughter' and the lower trigram is Thunder – 'the eldest son'. One element of the Judgement on this reading is that the stronger has placed itself below the weaker 'in order to obtain a following'. Another comes from the attributes of the two trigrams, The Arousing has placed itself below The Joyous. Both these images convey the idea of a couple it would be advantageous to follow. The pairing of strength and weakness, arousing and joyous, is felicitous and should produce a movement worth following.

THE COMPLETE LIST OF METAPHORICAL ATTRIBUTES OF THE EIGHT TRIGRAMS.

The idea of 'the family' explored above is just the tip of the metaphorical iceberg. Confucius (or his circle) went on to ascribe a long list of attributes to each trigram in turn. The point of this, of course, is to open as many conduits as possible into our unconscious, just as our dreams offer. It says a lot for these early Chinese insights into our unconscious minds that the same metaphors work today for people of all races and cultures. The complete list runs as follows.

1) ☰ The Creative: Heaven.

The Creative is heaven. It is round, it is the prince, the father, jade, metal, cold, ice; it is deep red, a good horse, an old horse, a wild horse, tree fruit. Later commentaries add to the list: *it is straight, it is the dragon, the upper garment, the word.*

Main attribute: strength. Associated animal: horse.

Remember that what the I Ching is always doing is providing a way into our unconscious, so all these metaphorical attributes are the sorts of images the unconscious has for the abstract concept of The Creative. They are dream images for dreams about creativity. Jade, for instance, is spotlessly pure and firm, as is metal. Cold and ice likewise hint at purity, impartiality, objectivity. Deep red is an enigmatic image: wouldn't deep blue accord more with Heaven? But perhaps deep red speaks of passion, blood, and hence creativity. Horses of various sorts appear in many of the lists. I suppose 2,500 years ago horses were much more a part of human day-to-day existence, and hence a more potent image. The adjectives are the important element, denoting, respectively, power, endurance, firmness and strength. (The 'wild' horse in Chinese fable is a mythical saw-toothed creature, able to tear even a tiger to pieces.)

2) ☷ ☷ *The receptive: Earth*

The Receptive is the earth, the mother. It is cloth, a kettle, frugality; it is level, a cow with a calf, a large wagon, form, the multitude, a shaft. Among the various kinds of soil it is the black.

   Main attribute: yielding. Associated animal: cow.

Again, most of these are readily clear as unconscious images of receptivity, motherhood, nurturing life. The earth is 'clothed' with life; a kettle or boiling pot provides nourishment. Mothers are frugal, used to making the best of little. They treat all their children impartially – they are 'level'. A cow with calf shows fertility; a large wagon carries much, just as the earth carries all living things. Form has overtones of ornamentation, as opposed to the brute 'content' that belongs to the Creative. Likewise, the Earth is plural, containing the 'multitude', unlike the singularity of the creative. The shaft is the body of the tree, the trunk, that bears all the various branches, and black soil is the most fertile.

3) ☳ ☳ *The Arousing: Thunder*

The arousing is thunder, the dragon. It is dark yellow, a spreading out, a great road, the eldest son. It is decisive and vehement; it is bamboo that is green and young, it is reed and rush. Among horses it signifies those which can neigh well, those with white hind legs, those which gallop, those with a star on the forehead. And among useful plants it is the pod-bearing ones. Finally, it is the strong, that which grows luxuriantly.

Main attribute: movement. Associated animal: dragon.

All these images conjure up strength and explosivity. Bamboo, reed and rush thrust upwards, pod-bearing plants literally explode to release their seeds. Dark yellow is a moody colour, signifying strong emotion – jealousy, envy, a jaundiced outlook on life. A spreading out suggests the rapid creep of foliage in spring, and a great road is a main artery. The various horses named are the extroverts, with the loud neighs, the white hind legs gleam from afar as they gallop, as does the star on the forehead. Galloping itself is the strongest and most explosive of the gaits.

4) ☴ *The Gentle: Wood or Wind*

The gentle is wood, wind, the eldest daughter, the guideline, work. It is the white, the long, the high; it is advance and retreat, the undecided, scent or odour. Among men it means the grey-haired, those with broad foreheads; it means those with much white in their eyes; it means those who gain, so that in the market they get threefold value. Finally, it is the sign of vehemence.

Main attribute: penetration. Associated animal: the cock.

There is an element in this image of 'getting things done, quietly but efficiently' Wood grows organically, the wind drives sails and windmills invisibly, but effectively. White is quintessentially Yin, and in a sense so is this eldest daughter. Her way of working is the Yin way, quiet and effective. Wood and wind both grow and blow long and high, but both are changeable, growing and blowing in varying directions: hence the idea of advance and retreat, and the undecided. Scent is carried on the wind, and the various woods each have their own distinctive odours. 'Grey-haired and broad foreheads' refers to the elderly, who tend perhaps to be gentler, and to work more quietly. But they have learnt guile, and are consummate bargainers. Much white in the eyes moves us on to arrogance and aggression, vehemence, so that, rather unexpectedly, the eldest daughter can be as forceful as her brother, Thunder. To repeat, do remember we are dealing in unconscious images, pictures that well up in us as representations of these fundamental archetypes.

5) ☵ The Abysmal: Water

The abysmal is water, ditches, ambush, bending and straightening out, bow and wheel. Among men it means the melancholy, those with sick hearts, those with earache. It is the blood sign; it is red. Among horses it means those with beautiful backs, those with wild courage, those which let their hair hang, those with thin hoofs, those which stumble. Among chariots it means those with many defects. It is penetration, the moon. It means thieves. Among varieties of wood it means those which are firm and have much pith.

Main attribute: dangerous. Associated animal: pig.

There are two main images at play here; connected but separate. Firstly the image of menace, danger, and imperfection: secondly the image of penetration, which comes because the single Yang line 'penetrates' the two Yin lines. In some ways these are both typical of the 'second son'. He comes between the eldest and the youngest; he has to resort to guile to assert his place in the family – neither the looked-for first-born nor the adored youngest.

The first set are clear enough – the various attributes of water and of danger. The one strong line 'hemmed-in' by the Yin lines suggests melancholy, a feeling of being trapped, being sick at heart. Earache is an unreachable pain, one which can't be scratched or relieved. Red appears again, this time as the universal colour for danger. The various horses slyly suggest dangerous women, with beautiful backs, luxuriant hair, but hiding serious defects – thin hoofs and a proclivity to stumble. Likewise, the chariot is not one to buy.

The last set of images refer to penetration; thieves break in, steal, then melt away. Pith penetrates the core of weak woods like elder or bamboo. The moon in this context signifies night, a dangerous time. And yet there is often an element of escape from danger in the readings where this trigram is a part, an escape in the way that water escapes from every obstacle that would interrupt its flow: by building up slowly and overwhelming the obstacle, and so moving on inexorably towards its goal, the sea.

6) ☲ The Clinging: Fire

The Clinging is fire, the sun, lightning, the middle daughter. It means coats of mail and helmets, lances and weapons. Among men it means the big-bellied. It is the sign of dryness. It means the tortoise, the crab, the snail, the mussel, the hawkbill tortoise. Among trees it means those which dry out in the upper part of the trunk.

> *Main attribute: dependence. Associated animal: pheasant.*

Here the unconscious image is of warmth, comfort, the womb even, to which we cling instinctively. The armaments are defensive, presenting a firm outer shell protecting a soft and vulnerable inside: as of course are the tortoise, the crab, the snail etc. This is suggested by the trigram itself, where two strong Yang lines protect the yielding Yin line between them. But there is, as ever, the attendant risk of drying out, becoming nothing but the dry husk, as shown by the dying tree, where the upper part is senescent.

7) ☶ Keeping still: The Mountain

Keeping still is the mountain; it is a bypath; it means little stones, doors and openings, fruits and seeds, eunuchs and watchmen, the fingers. It is the dog, the rat and the various types of black-billed birds. Among trees it signifies the firm and gnarled (e.g. hawthorn).

> *Main attribute: standstill. Associated animal: dog.*

Here the underlying unconscious image is of guarding, holding fast, protecting, watching. Safety is achieved by keeping still and watchful. The trigram's shape suggests doors and openings, and even the mountain itself. The seed, left quietly to mature, becomes the fruit – which in its turn contains the seed, all in a still fashion. Fingers hold fast, dogs guard, the rat gnaws, black-billed birds grip easily, and gnarled trunks grow slowly but have great strength. Throughout there is a picture of holding on to what we have, in an understated way.

8) ☱ The Joyous: The Lake

The joyous is the lake, the youngest daughter. It is a sorceress; it is a mouth and tongue. It means smashing and breaking apart; dropping off and bursting open. Among the kinds of soil it is the hard and salty. Among animals it is the sheep or goat.

Main attribute: pleasure. Associated animal: sheep.

The fundamental image here is of fulfilment: hence the joy. Lake is placed at Autumn on the New Family diagram, a time of gathering, of fruitfulness. But there is an element of harshness here too, of destruction in the gathering. This is often true of comedy, there is joy and laughter, but it is often cruel and destructive.

The youngest daughter is a great joy in a family, but she often grows up craftily, having seen the ways of both older sisters and brothers. Hence the idea of a sorceress, who speaks often in riddles. The shape of the trigram apparently suggested an open, speaking, mouth to the Chinese, with the tongue as the middle line. It also suggested a ram's or goat's head, with the horns. Hence the animal image. Autumn's fruit often falls to the ground and bursts open. A dried-up lake leaves hard, salty soil, but good soil nevertheless, with lots of silt. This is typical of the whole philosophy. Basically this trigram is the Joyous, but joy contains the seeds of cruelty, hurt and pain within it.

Before we move on to consider the complexities of the hexagrams, let's just recapitulate on the point of all these metaphors, at least from a Western point of view. We are affirming that the way the I Ching works is to put our conscious minds in touch with what our unconscious already knows about any situation we find ourselves in. If we could remember and interpret our dreams they would do the same task, and the interpretation would involve understanding the metaphors and puns that dreams use. An I Ching reading lists a complex set of metaphors which, interpreted correctly, shed light on the situation we are in. Originally in Chinese simply the metaphors themselves were given in response to the hexagram generated, together with the six possible degrees of change if one or more 'moving Yang' or 'moving Yin' lines had been cast, and by meditating on the metaphors the client could unlock his own unconscious to help with his problem or question. The Confucian school amplified the metaphors, and their interpretations have stood the test of time. However, if we Westerners could learn to interpret the metaphors for ourselves we might well find the meaning clearer, even if the process took a little longer.

With that in mind, let's just take one example of a reading simply with the original Chinese translated, but without Wilhelm's translation of the commentary, to see if the sense is there anyway, without help. At random, let's go for Reading 36: Darkening of the light.

Darkening of the light: No. 36

THE CONDITION

The sun (the bottom trigram, Fire) has gone below the Earth (the top trigram). The light has, quite literally, been darkened.

THE JUDGEMENT

In adversity, it favours one to be persevering.

THE IMAGE

The light has sunk into the earth;
The image of darkening of the light.
Thus does the superior man live with the great mass;
He veils his light, and yet it shines.

The six degrees of change (starting as always with the bottom line) are given thus:

1) Moving Yang at the beginning means:
Darkening of the light during flight.
He lowers his wings.
The superior man does not eat for three days

On his wanderings.
But he has somewhere to go.
The host has occasion to gossip about him.

2) Moving Yin in the second line means:
    Darkening of the light injures him in the left thigh.
    He gives aid with the strength of a horse.
    Good fortune.

3) Moving Yang in the third line means:
    Darkening of the light during the hunt in the south.
    Their great leader is captured.
    One must not expect perseverance too soon.

4) Moving Yin in the fourth line means:
    He penetrates the left side of the belly.
    One gets at the very heart of the darkening of the light,
    And leaves gate and courtyard.

5) Moving Yin in the fifth line means:
    Darkening of the light as with Prince Chi.
    Perseverance furthers.

6) Moving Yin in the top line means:
    Not light but darkness.
    First he climbed up to heaven,
    Then he plunged into the depths of the earth.

Well, let's be honest, without any commentary these are pretty difficult to make sense of, but let's give it a try. **THE CONDITION** is obvious enough, without any commentary. The sun has set, day has become night: and the metaphor that we are now in dark times is easy. Just given the bare **JUDGEMENT**, we can apply our own understanding: it has become night, but in time it will become day again, and the light will return, so persevere. And the **IMAGE** makes it clear that we will have a hard time of it, but must nevertheless try to bring our own, veiled, light onto the situation. "It is better to light a single candle than to sit and curse the dark". The degrees of change are a bit harder.

1) Presumably we have been 'flying high', succeeding, when suddenly it's all gone belly up. Stop flying, take stock, rein in, consolidate. Nevertheless, we do have something to offer, and should do so, even if others make fun and gossip about us.

2) Whatever has happened has wounded us, but not fatally. (The left thigh is not our strongest, and contains no vital organs.) We are still able to help the cause… or is it that the strong horse will come to our aid?

3) 'During the hunt in the south'. What can we make of that unaided? Perhaps nothing, but it is clear that if their great leader has been captured (presumably the opposition's) things should improve. Why then should we not 'expect perseverance too soon'? I suppose this is a warning that although we seem to have made a breakthrough in the dark times it is still far off morning. (The hunt was 'in the south', not in the east, where morning might be expected soon?). In other words, 'one swallow does not a summer make', we will have to persevere a long time still.

4) This one is a serious injury, perhaps even fatal. We have confronted the source of the evil that has brought dark times, and we have not prevailed: indeed, we have been badly hurt. It is time to retreat, to 'leave both gate and courtyard'.

5) Without some hints as to who Prince Chi was, this is impenetrable. Apparently he lived at the court of a tyrant who was his uncle. Unable to leave he concealed his distress at his uncle's barbarity and feigned insanity, in much the same way as Hamlet. Knowing that, perhaps we can work out for ourselves that we are 'between a rock and a hard place'. No path leads out, so we must take any possible steps to preserve ourselves, however mad the world thinks us.

6) Could we work out for ourselves that this is a hopeful change? It is reminding us that just as the sun, light, climbed into the heavens and then plunged into darkness,

so too this dark night has climbed high, but will also plunge into morning, and the return of the light.

I do think it may be more helpful and more satisfying to try to see what the bare Chinese Condition, Judgement, Image and Degrees of Change say to us before reading Wilhelm's amplified commentary, though I accept he always has something new and helpful to add after we have given it a go ourselves.

Just given the hexagram, and splitting it into its two constituent trigrams, we could find various other metaphors, using the lists above of the meanings contained in Earth and Fire. For instance, why should we not use others of the given images, and see the image as that of a hard-shelled nut, say an acorn, buried in the depths of the earth? Actually, of course, the interpretation would be similar. For the present, there is no light, and the nut seems to have perished. But given time, and perseverance, it will grow, poke through the earth into the light, and eventually become a mighty oak.

Alternatively, we could posit the 'middle daughter' chafing under the rule of her mother: both valid images of ⚏ and ☲ respectively. But again, we would find the same judgement valid: the middle daughter needs to persevere and she will eventually grow and leave the family home, and blossom in her own right.

Continuing the possible interpretations, we could say the *'coats of mail and helmets, lances and weapons'* had been hidden under *'the cloth'*. Well, once again, the meaning is similar: they are out of use for now, but their time will come again, when the cloth will be lifted, and the armaments girded on again.

So perhaps it is as well to go with the wisdom of the ages and use the image, condition and judgement of the ancients, translated into our own times.

DIFFERENT TYPES OF INTERPRETATIONS OF THE HEXAGRAMS

We can classify the various types of interpretation and learn a little of the many ways our unconscious can make itself felt. There turn out to be several different types.

Main name interpretations.

As we have seen above, some hexagrams are interpreted using their main names, and the positions, above or below. The Fire/Sun has gone beneath the Earth leads naturally to the 'Darkening of the light'. Other examples we have already met were No. 16, Enthusiasm, The Arousing (Thunder) followed by the Receptive (Earth) seemed a natural description of an enthusiasm… and its inverse, No. 24, The Turning Point seemed a fair interpretation of The Receptive followed by The Arousing.

Visual puns.

These interpretations depend on the very shape of the hexagram. As an example let's look at No. 27, Providing nourishment.

Providing nourishment. No. 27

As we can see, the visual pun is obvious, the hexagram looks like a wide open mouth, ready to be fed. (Or perhaps an empty stomach.) In construction terms it is Mountain above Thunder. The attributes of Mountain are *Keeping still is the mountain; it is a bypath; it means little stones, doors and openings, fruits and seeds, eunuchs and watchmen, the fingers. It is the dog, the rat and the various types of black-billed birds. Among trees it signifies the firm and gnarled (e.g. hawthorn).*

And of Thunder are *The arousing is thunder, the dragon. It is dark yellow, a spreading out, a great road, the eldest son. It is decisive and vehement; it is bamboo that is green and young, it is reed and rush. Among horses it signifies those which can neigh well, those with white hind legs, those which gallop, those with a star on the forehead. And among useful plants it is the pod-bearing ones. Finally, it is the strong, that which grows luxuriantly.*

In the original Chinese the hexagram is interpreted thus:

THE CONDITION

Providing nourishment represents the nourishment and care of oneself and also of others in a higher, spiritual sense.

THE JUDGEMENT

> *Perseverance brings good fortune.*
> *Pay heed to the providing of nourishment*
> *And to what a man seeks*
> *To fill his mouth with.*

THE IMAGE

> *At the foot of the mountain, thunder:*
> *The image of providing nourishment.*
> *Thus the superior man is careful of his words*
> *And temperate in eating and drinking.*

If we were to look first at 'Keeping Still' above 'The Arousing' I suppose we might posit a condition of taking care no matter what the stimulus, and perhaps a judgement such as "Do not allow arousal and excitement to cloud your judgement. Keep still and weigh the stimulus up carefully before accepting it". Perhaps not too far from the real judgement?

If we considered the 'doors and openings' attribute of Mountain as above the idea of luxuriant growth inherent in Thunder I suppose we move towards the idea of food passing into an opening – the mouth? Likewise I suppose 'the fingers' dipping into 'pod-bearing plants' conjures up an image of feeding.

Nevertheless, it does seem that we are straining to fit images to the 'official' Chinese interpretation. I don't know why they decided that this hexagram (and several others) should be interpreted as visual puns, but certainly the idea that some should be is reasonable. Our dreams are often puns, visual and verbal, and make their point in that fashion. All we can say as Western observers is that this is the interpretation given in this case, and it has stood the test of time, and still today can give meaning and substance to a unconscious image.

Another example of the 'Visual Pun Interpretation' is No. 28,

Great heaviness where the image is of a beam, thick in the

middle but thin at the ends, bending and breaking under its own weight.

On a similar theme, No. 62, Great smallness ☷☳ is said to resemble a bird in flight, and the situation is one where, in contrast, the danger is in trying to fly too high.

Moving away from each other.

Quite frequently an interpretation takes some of its power from the idea that the upper trigram is rising while the lower one is sinking. The two are moving apart, which can be good or bad depending on what the trigrams represent. Take for instance No. 6, Conflict ☰☵ where **THE CONDITION** says

> *Heaven's nature is to rise upwards, while Water's nature is to flow downwards. The trigram's tendencies are to move away from each other; hence the idea of conflict.*

There are two other elements to **THE CONDITION** that reinforce this concept:

> *The trigrams' attributes are danger (inner guile) and strength. Where cunning has force before it there is conflict.* And

> *In terms of character, inner cunning and fixed outward determination indicate a person who is sure to be quarrelsome.*

This example, then, uses three different images to make the same point. The unconscious is hammering on the door of the conscious!

On the other hand, in No. 40, Deliverance ☳☵ the movement is said to take us out of the sphere of danger. The upper trigram, Thunder (The Arousing) denotes upward movement while the lower, Water (The Abysmal) flows downwards, giving the idea of release from the tension.

Clearly, this all requires careful thought, but seen as ways the unconscious communicates with the conscious, as for instance in dreams, the interpretations are reasonable.

Moving towards each other.

Similarly, if the upper trigram is held to be a 'sinking' type, and the lower a 'rising' type, the result can be good or bad. The best example of this type of interpretation is for No. 3, Resolving Chaos ䷂. Here the lower trigram, Thunder, is rising, pushing upwards, while the upper trigram, Water, is flowing downwards. Here THE CONDITION claims that *the Abysmal sinks, the upward Arousing movement passes through it to beyond the danger.* There seems to be a great deal of random decision as to what is good and what is bad movement! However, centuries of honing the interpretations does seem persuasive..

Position of a particular line.

Quite frequently an interpretation depends on a particular line in a particular position – especially if it is the only Yang line, or the only Yin line. An example of this is No. 44, Encountering (Coming to meet) ䷫. Here THE CONDITION states that *the hexagram represents a situation where the dark principle (the Yin line), after having been eliminated, furtively and unexpectedly re-enters from within and below. The situation is unfavourable and dangerous. We must understand it and promptly prevent the possible consequences.*

In No. 19, Approach (Becoming great) ䷒ the two Yang lines are held to be 'growing into the hexagram' from within. Their light-giving power expands with them.

Attribute interpretations.

Very similar to 'Main name' interpretations, but these use different attributes of the trigrams to derive a meaning. Indeed, often it is both the names and the attributes that combine to reinforce the meaning. Take for example, No. 4 Immaturity (Youthful folly) ䷃. Here the image is of a stream issuing at the foot of a mountain. Which way shall it go? The attributes agree: danger after standstill (Water under Mountain) suggests perplexity.

No. 5, Waiting, ䷄ uses the same dual technique. The image is of clouds (Water) in the Heavens – implying waiting for rain: and the attributes are of strength within danger. As in a game of chess, for instance, strength, in the face of danger, bides its time, and does not go rushing in.

There seems to me to be something very satisfying when several aspects of a hexagram point in the same direction. It is as if several dreams occur, one after another, all trying to get the same message from the unconscious to the conscious.

Physical positioning of elements.

This is very similar to the first type, where the main names suggest the interpretation, but in the case, for instance, of No. 48, The Well ䷯, the wood is seen as a wooden bucket, physically lowered into water, in order to fill and bring it up from the well. This is a very powerful image.

Imagining a line has moved.

This is a pretty specialised sort of interpretation, and is applied, for instance, both in No. 41, Decrease ䷨ and No. 42 Increase ䷩. The reasoning goes, for No. 41, The lower trigram has, as it were lost a strong (Yang) line to the upper, decreasing the strength of the foundations in favour of the superstructure. Vice versa for No. 42.

Doubled trigrams.

As might be expected, when a hexagram is formed by a repeated trigram, the meaning is that of the single trigram, but emphatically. There are of course eight of these. Let's take No. 52 Keeping Still ䷳, Mountain over Mountain, as an example.

THE CONDITION reads *'Here the image of a Mountain is doubled. It is at rest because the Yang principle, which strives upwards, is at the top, while the Yin principle, whose nature is to move downwards, is below. It is the rest of movement that has reached its natural end.'*

Here, then, we have nine different ways of interpreting hexagrams. There must be at least as many ways our unconscious tries to get in touch with our conscious minds. Dreams themselves use many of the above methods. One interesting method I find in my own life is that a fragment of a song will pop into my head, and I'll find myself humming, singing or whistling it, only to find that it contains an appropriate line for the current situation. It's not earth-shattering, but it is an example of the constant interplay between the various different parts of our brains.

Chapter six

The degrees of change

THE MYRIAD FACTORS IN THE DEGREES OF CHANGE

We have seen in chapter five that many different ways are used to interpret the basic reading. Each reading, remember, has six degrees of change attached, each relating to a 'moving Yang' line or 'moving Yin' line. These 'changing lines' have their own very complex litany of interpretations.

Firm and yielding lines, superior and inferior positions.

For obvious reasons, a Yang line is regarded as being 'firm' (male, aggressive etc.) while a Yin line is regarded as 'yielding'. For reasons that needn't concern us, the positions of a line, reading up from the bottom, came to be regarded as 'superior' if they were odd, and 'inferior' if they were even. This allows for four possibilities: a line can be firm in a superior position (Yang in line 1, 3 or 5); firm in an inferior position (Yang in line 2, 4 or 6); yielding in a superior position (Yin in line 1, 3 or 5) or Yin in an inferior position (Yin in line 2,4 or 6). Yang in a superior position and Yin in an inferior position are regarded as 'correct', and otherwise as 'not correct'. Generally, a line moving from a correct position to an incorrect signals misfortune, and vice versa signals good fortune.

A 'moving Yang' line which is, in the hexagram under investigation, in a superior position will change to a Yin line in that superior position. This is generally (but not always) interpreted as misfortune, since Yang in superior, Yin in inferior, is seen as the equilibrium position. (That is, both are in their 'correct' positions as defined above). Taking the example No. 35, Easy progress, with its hexagram Fire over Earth, if it had moving Yin at the second line and moving Yang at the sixth, would move to ䷧, Thunder over Water, No. 40, which is Deliverance.

Here Moving Yin is in the second (inferior) line and is going to become Yang in an inferior position: this is generally seen as an unfortunate change, and indeed, the reading runs thus.

2) Progressing, but frustrated. Persevere
When progress is halted because we are kept from getting in touch with the man in authority with whom we have an affinity, we must remain persevering, despite our sorrow. In the end great happiness will be bestowed; and be well-deserved, being based not on selfish or partisan motives, but on firm and correct principles.

As can be seen, from 'Easy progress' this is decidedly a setback, but not fatal. We will return to the image of 'affinity with the man in authority' very soon.

On the other hand, the Moving Yang is in position 6, a firm line in an inferior position, which will move to the more favourable Yin in an inferior position. We would expect this to be a favourable change, and indeed the judgement is that too much aggression (yang) is a danger.

6) Progress by force. Beware of danger.
Forceful progress is permissible only in dealing with the mistakes of one's own people. Even then we must bear in mind its dangers, if we are to avoid mistakes. To persist too energetically, especially with those with whom we have no close connection, will lead to humiliation. Forceful progress is dangerous.

Nuclear trigrams.
These are an example of how convoluted the whole study of the hexagrams became. Somewhere along the line practitioners decided that any hexagram contained, as well as the two trigrams that form it (top three lines and bottom three lines), also two 'nuclear trigrams', that is two trigrams embedded within the hexagram. These were

defined as lines 3,4 and 5 as the 'upper nuclear trigram' and lines 2,3 and 4 as the 'lower nuclear trigram'. As an example, consider the hexagram ䷥, Fire above Lake, No. 38, Opposition. The 'upper nuclear trigram' is made of lines 3,4 and 5, and is therefore ☵, Water, and the 'lower nuclear trigram' is made up of lines 2,3 and 4 and is therefore ☲, Fire again. The opposition between Fire and Water is therefore reinforced, appearing in the hexagram as Fire and Lake and again in the nuclear trigrams. However, this is not the point as far as we are concerned here. The point is, that if we delve into nuclear trigrams, lines 3 and 4 become very important, as they are part of both the original hexagram and <u>both</u> the nuclear trigrams. Line 5 is part of the upper nuclear trigram and the original hexagram, and similarly line 2 is part of the lower nuclear trigram and the original hexagram. Therefore line 1 and line 6 tend to drop out of the connection, while a state of equilibrium, usually favourable, exists between line 2 and line 5, each appearing twice. The two middle lines, 3 and 4, each belong to both nuclear trigrams which disturbs their balance in all but the most favourable cases. These relationships correspond exactly with the evaluation of the lines in the appended judgements.

King Wen's influence.

The lines of change and their associated judgements came in with the beginning of the Zhou Dynasty, starting with King Wen, who lived about 1150 B.C., and his son the Duke of Zhou. Wen was imprisoned for a long time at the hands of the tyrant Zhou Hsin, and this experience pervades the meaning of the lines. The Duke of Zhou decided the lines corresponded to various officials at court. In this scenario, lines 2 and 5 are the most important, being the central lines in their trigrams. These are taken to convey the correct relationship of official to ruler, son to father, wife to husband. If the second line is strong (Yang) and the fifth line yielding (Yin), the result is favourable. For example, in Reading No. 4, Youthful immaturity, the hexagram is , Mountain over Water. Here the 2nd line is Yang, the 5th is Yin, and the corresponding degrees of change read as follows:

2) To bear with fools kindly brings favour.

We need inner strength rather than external power to bear our burden of responsibility and tolerate, with kindliness, the shortcomings of human folly. Like a son, required to take charge of the household, we must show chivalrous consideration towards the weaker. It is only inner strength and outer reserve that enable us to take on social responsibilities with success.

5) Childlike folly brings good fortune.

An inexperienced person who seeks instruction in a childlike and unassuming way is on the right path. Someone who is devoid of arrogance, gentle, devoted and ready to listen, who subordinates himself, will surely be helped.

Both these degrees of change are favourable, and use the image, in the first, of a strong son or official, and in the second of a yielding ruler, prepared to learn. (But note that the strong 2nd line is in an inferior position, and the yielding 5th line in a superior position, as defined above. The favourability is justified when they are moving lines as they will change to the 'correct' positions.)

Line 4, the bottom line of the upper trigram, is taken to represent a minister who is close to the ruler (who is line 5). Line 3, the highest line in the lower trigram, holds a sort of transitional position. In this example, line 4 is Yin in an inferior position, which is a favourable position. A change will not then be favourable, and The Degree of Change reads:

4) Entangled folly brings humiliation.

The minister is hopelessly entangled in empty imaginings and is obstinately preoccupied with unreal fantasies. He should be left to himself for a while and not spared the humiliation that ensues.

Also in this example, line 3 (the transient position) is Yin in a superior position but this time the reading looks at its change to say it is unfavourable. There is certainly no rigid adherence to any rules! The reading runs

3) Like a foolish girl one loses oneself.

Like a foolish girl, throwing herself away, a weak, immature man, struggling to rise, can easily lose his own individuality by slavishly imitating a stronger personality of higher station.

The Time.

The situation represented by the hexagram as a whole is called 'the Time', and it can have entirely different meanings according to the character of the various hexagrams.

1) Where the situation has to do with movement, 'the Time' means the decrease or growth, the emptiness or fullness, brought about by this movement. Examples are: Peace (No. 11); Standstill (No. 12); Splitting apart (No. 23) and Return (No. 24).

2) Where the situation is an action or a process, that is called 'the Time'. Examples are: Conflict (6); The Army (7); Biting through (21) and Providing Nourishment (27).

3) Sometimes 'the Time' refers to the law expressed in a hexagram, as in: Conduct (10); Modesty (15); Influence (31) and Duration (32).

4) Lastly, 'the Time' may mean the symbolic situation represented by the hexagram, as in : The Well (48) and The Cauldron (50).

In all cases the 'Time' of a hexagram determines the meaning of the situation as a whole, on the basis of which the individual lines receive their meaning. Any given line may be favourable or unfavourable according to the Time determinant.

The relationship of the lines to each other.

This is, in the light of chapter seven, a fascinating connection for the original commentators to have brought to light. Lines occupying analogous places in the lower and upper trigrams sometimes have an especially close relationship: that of correspondence. That is, the first line corresponds with the fourth; the second with the fifth; and the third with the sixth. We have already seen that lines 2 and 5 frequently have a strong connection, and the same is true to a lesser extent for 1 and 4, 3 and 6. Wilhelm in his definitive translation notes this correspondence is most likely when one of the pair is Yang, the other Yin. This he terms a 'stable correspondence'. We will return to this concept in chapter seven.

The numbers applying to the lines.

This is fundamental to the Chinese system of generating the lines. It is arcane, and yet will turn out, when we look at the relationship to DNA, to have an astonishing modern connection. If the lines are being generated by coin tossing a Head is given the value 3, and a tail the value 2. This harks back to the original method of divination, separating yarrow stalks, which is covered in chapter nine.

Therefore: 3 heads gives Moving Yang and counts 3+3+3=9

3 tails gives moving yin and counts 2+2+2=6

1 head and 2 tails gives Yang, and counts 3+2+2=7

2 heads and 1 tail gives yin and counts 3+3+2=8

Remember, this annotation is over 3,000 years old. How utterly amazing then that these totals should prove to be the key that helps unlock the exact parallel between the I Ching and DNA. Again, we will return to this in chapter seven.

The special value attached to line 6.

Line 6 is held to be, in a sense, 'outside' the situation. The worldly aspects of the situation have often been dealt with by lines 1 to 5. Line 6 often pertains to 'the sage who is no longer involved in worldly affairs or an eminent man who is without power' (*Wilhelm p. 291*). Again, this has an astonishing echo in DNA theory, which, yet again, we will return to in chapter seven.

All in all, the various 'degrees of change' lines can accord to a huge variety of factors, and it is not possible to pre-determine which of the many possible factors will have been chosen by the original philosophers: but they will accord to one or more of the above variants. Just why one is chosen over another is not always explicable, but I come back, as ever, to the experiential fact that 'it works'.

AN EXAMPLE OF THE FORCES AT WORK IN THE DEGREES OF CHANGE.

To see how the factors above work out in practice, let's look at Reading No. 50, The Great Bowl. Its hexagram is ☲☴, Fire over Wood.

THE CONDITION

The image of fire, kindled by wood, suggests the preparation of food, and the heart of the home. Here it symbolises the ceremonial vessel used to hold food for sacred rites and banquets, and for family meals. It is shaped as a great bronze bowl, with legs, handles and carrying rings. It was from such a bowl the head of the house would serve his honoured guests.

THE JUDGEMENT

> *The Great Bowl: supreme good fortune.*
> *Herein lies the culmination of culture,*
> *Enlightenment and true understanding:*
> *Clarity comes through inner gentleness.*

In reality, food was not cooked in this great vessel, but was served up in it on religious and special occasions. Here, all that is best in Man is celebrated: his generosity to others and his sacrifice and worship of 'God', the Other, whatever you want to call the numinous power behind life.

THE IMAGE

> *Fire over wood;*
> *The image of the cauldron.*
> *Thus the superior man consolidates his fate*
> *By making his position correct.*

The symbolism here is that, just as the wood under a fire needs constantly to be replenished, so a wise man continuously consolidates his position and feeds the projects that nourish him.

Reading, from the bottom up as always, the Degrees of Change are as follows.

1) A great bowl, upturned for cleaning.
The lowly are honoured for their work.

There is a visual pun in the hexagram, where the whole is shaped somewhat like a great bowl: the bottom (Yin) line represents the legs it stands on; the next three lines are the body of the cauldron; the fifth line, with its hole, represents the 'ears' or handle of the cauldron; and the sixth the lid. This first line, as so often the 'least important', refers to lowly people – those who clean out the bowl – affirming that their work is nevertheless important, and so are they.

2) There is good food in one's great bowl.
But one is envied. Be cautious. No blame.

The line is firm and central to the lower trigram, and as it forms the pictorial body of the cauldron along with lines 3 & 4, it is linked to them. However, it is also, as so often, primarily linked to line 5, the 'ruler' of the hexagram; the more so as it is Yang and line 5 is Yin, and so the servant will suffer no harm even though those around are envious, for the prince will protect him.

3) The handle of the cauldron is bent, or altered.
One is impeded in his way of life.
The fat of the pheasant is not eaten.
Once rain falls, remorse is spent.
Good fortune comes at the end.

I defy anyone to work this one out unaided! All sorts of the myriad factors are at play. Firstly, although it is line 5 which represents the 'ears' of the cauldron, these ears have carrying ring on them that 'hang down' as far as line 3. The picture is of an overturned cauldron, where the carrying handle gave way spilling the plump pheasant within, and thus spoiling the feast. Hence the idea of being impeded.

104

Why a pheasant? Perhaps because, when line 3 changes to Yin the lower <u>nuclear</u> trigram changes to Fire, whose symbolic animal is the pheasant.

However, all is not lost, because the Upper nuclear trigram is just coming into view (line 3 is its lowest line) and it is ☱, the Joyous Lake. Not only so, but as the line changes to Yin, so the upper nuclear trigram becomes Water, or rain in this case – and so does the original lower trigram, reinforcing the idea of refreshing rain!

> *4) The legs of the cauldron are broken.*
> *The prince's meal is spilled*
> *And his person is soiled.*
> *Misfortune.*

Why the legs? Because line 4 corresponds to line 1, as they are of opposite polarity, and line 1 was the legs. Also, line 4 is subservient to line 5, the prince or ruler of the hexagram, so the broken leg is seen as spilling the contents over one's prince… who had been invited as honoured guest. Misfortune indeed.

> *5) The great bowl has yellow handles, golden carrying rings.*
> *Perseverance furthers one.*
> *The yellow handles of the cauldron are central, in order to receive*
> *what is real.*

This is symbolism of the highest order. Yellow is the colour of the middle way (the central colour of the light spectrum), and gold emphasises it. Line 5 makes the upper trigram hollow, or receptive. Line 5 is the ruler, or prince's line. What is being suggested is that he will find strong and able helpers if he is approachable, receptive to ideas, modest, and seeks wise counsel. (From the sage, at line 6, who is above him). When it changes, the upper trigram becomes the Creative, with all that implies. Also, the upper nuclear trigram is Lake, which has, surprisingly, metal among its attributes, and the symbolism is (apparently!) that when the line changes from Yin =yielding, to Yang = firm, then the golden (ceremonial) handles will be replaced by the real hard metal handles and so can be carried.

6) The great bowl has carrying handles of Jade.
Great good fortune.
Nothing that would act to further.
The jade rings in the highest place show the firm and the yielding
complementing each other properly.

This is similar to the situation in line 5, except that in that case it applied to the ruler, or prince, whereas in line 6 it applies to the sage: the wise man advising the prince. Instead of the firm metal that appeared in line 5, here the carrying rings are of precious jade. Our equivalent would be 'pearls of wisdom'. The sage is wise indeed, and the country will be well-led by a prince who takes his advice.

Let me reiterate that what we are dealing with in this chapter are symbols, metaphors, puns and pictures which allow our unconscious mind to inform and restrain our conscious mind, ridden as it is with all sorts of emotions, schemes and neuroses. The situation is, in fact, not dissimilar to the relationship of lines 5 & 6. Line 6, the sage advisor, stands as our unconscious in relation to line 5, our conscious 'ruler'. The sage unconscious pricks our conscience, reminding the wayward, anarchic, self-focused conscious mind of the over-riding claims of society, responsibility, honour and proportionality.

Chapter seven

The exact correspondence between the I Ching hexagrams and our DNA

Before we can attempt to see the exact correspondence between the I Ching hexagrams and DNA and the production of amino acids, we need a very amateur, pictorial understanding of what is happening in our bodies all the time. Every cell in our bodies, and in the body of any living thing – plant, bacterium, virus or animal – contains a nucleus in which is packed a very tightly twisted strand of DNA. Every individual living entity has its own unique DNA. Here we are just interested in human DNA. If it were possible to unravel a strand it would be roughly 1.3 metres long, containing 48 chromosomes.

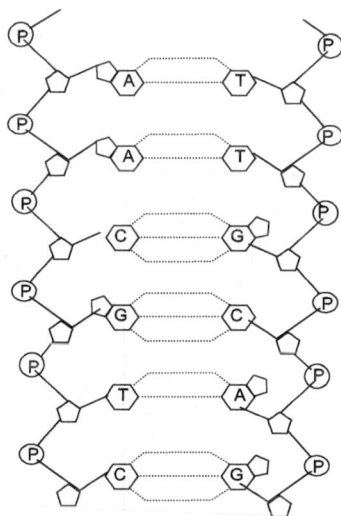

Essentially, this strand is just an immensely long list of paired chemical bases, and there are only four of them. Pictorially, a piece of the strand (straightened out) looks like a ladder, as shown here.
There are various things to note in this picture.

1) The four bases are called A (for Adenine), T (for Thymine), C (for Cytosine) and G (for Guanine).
2) A always binds to T, and T to A. C and G also always bond together.
3) A and G are 'double-ringed' and are called Purines.
4) T and C are 'single-ringed' pyrimidines.
5) There are two connections between A and T; three between C and G. (The dotted lines). These are hydrogen bonds, but that doesn't need to interest us.

There are in the order of 3 billion pairs of bases in each strand of DNA. The strand doesn't just sit there in the cell nucleus. The 'ladder' is continuously unzipped: indeed, it might be better to picture the two sides as interlinking sides of a zipper. Here's a simplistic picture of that unzipping.

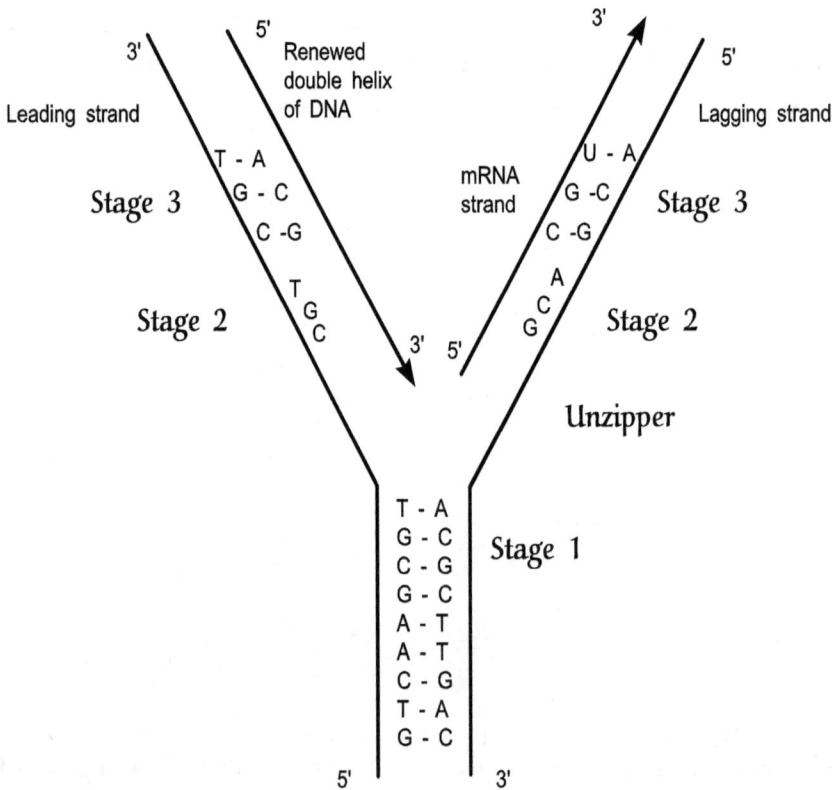

Things to note in this picture are:

1) Stage 1 is the 'zipped-up' double-sided DNA ladder. We are going to follow the top three pairs on their journey through the unzipper. We will refer to three pairs as a 'swatch': this

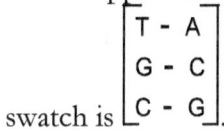

   swatch is
   $$\begin{bmatrix} T - A \\ G - C \\ C - G \end{bmatrix}.$$

2) You will notice 5' and 3' in various places. These are spoken of as 5 prime and 3 prime, and all we need to know about them is that they indicate the direction new bases must be added, and that opposite sides of the ladder go in opposite directions.

3) At Stage 2 the TGC side is called the Leading strand, and attracts the opposite bases immediately to produce a new complete strand of DNA, an exact copy of the original. The 'plan' is maintained. Because the new side is being written in the 5' to 3' direction it can happen immediately, so as each base is unzipped its complement is attached, as we see in Stage 3. We have no further interest in this strand.

4) At Stage 2 the ACG side is called the lagging strand, and it attracts its complementary side in a peculiar way. The complementary side is called mRNA (the m stands for messenger) but because it can only be written in the 5' to 3' direction it can only come in from behind, from the unzipper end, allowing the unattached lagging strand to build up somewhat before adding a piece of the mRNA. All we need for our purposes is to recognise that the mRNA builds up in the 'opposite' direction to the ACG, and so comes into the ribosome as CGU at Stage 3. (You would be expecting CGT, but for reasons that don't concern us the Thymine changes to Uracil in the mRNA, and so is written U) This CGU is called a Codon, and is what triggers the ribosome later to produce amino acids, which is what interests us.

This mRNA strand breaks away from the lagging strand to exist as a single independent, one-sided strand.

This long strand of mRNA which has built up in the 5' to 3' direction is eventually 'topped and tailed' and is then able to pass through the wall of the nucleus into the outer part of the cell, the 'workshop', where it will be read by many Ribosomes which take each three-letter codon and produce an appropriate amino acid. This can be pictured thus:

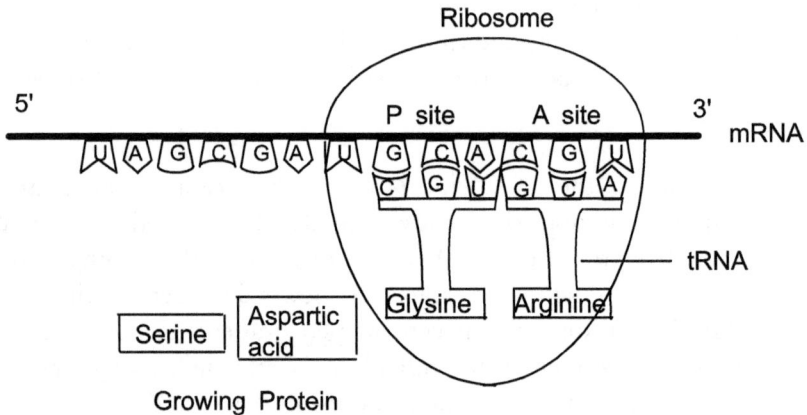

Things to note in this picture are:

The black line is the long strand of mRNA which was produced at Stage 3 of the previous picture. In simple terms, the ribosome (the heart-shaped blob above) moves along the mRNA strand (in the direction 5' to 3') taking three letters (a codon) at a time into its 'A site' which then attract their complement which is called tRNA. (The t stands for transitional). As the ribosome moves along this codon slips into the P site, and then is released, attached to the previous amino acid. It takes a long series of amino acids to build up a particular protein which is then used by the body. You can see in the picture that Serine and Aspartic Acid have already moved off, and that Glycine is about to join them, followed by the Arginine which has been attracted by our particular codon CGU.

THE STANDARD TABLE OF CODONS

There are 64 possible codons, since the first can be any of the four, U, C, A or G, as can the second, and the third. So there are 4x4x4=64 possibilities. There is a standard way of setting them out in an 8x8 matrix, which is done by listing the four in order down the side of the matrix; then along the top, then in each of the four sections down the right hand side. This gives the table:

Second base

		U	C	A	G	
First base	**U**	UUU Phenyl- UUC alanine UUA Leucine UUG	UCU UCC Serine UCA UCG	UAU Tyrosine UAC UAA Stop UAG Codons	UGU Cysteine UGC UGA Stop codon UGG Tryptophan	U C A G
	C	CUU CUC Leucine CUA CUG	CCU CCC Proline CCA CCG	CAU Histidine CAC CAA Glutamine CAG	CGU CGC Arginine CGA CGG	U C A G
	A	AUU AUC Isoleucine AUA AUG Met(Start)	ACU ACC Threonine ACA ACG	AAU Asparagine AAC AAA Lysine AAG	AGU Serine AGC AGA Arginine AGG	U C A G
	G	GUU GUC Valine GUA GUG	GCU GCC Alanine GCA GCG	GAU Aspartic GAC acid GAA Glutamic GAG acid	GGU GGC Glycine GGA GGG	U C A G

Third base

Things to note in this diagram

1) There are 20 amino acids produced, as named in the table, including Methionine – the 'start' codon.

2) These amino acids occur in blocks: many as a pair, some as groups of three, some four, and three of them, Serine, Leucine and Arginine, as a group of four and a separate group of two.

3) There are three 'Stop' codons, almost in a group.

THE VARIOUS 'CO-INCIDENCES' BETWEEN DNA AND THE I CHING.

Let me make clear from the start that I do not think these 'co-incidences' are accidental, in the sense that we usually place on the word coincidence, but that the patterns described happen in both disciplines because they are, in a very real sense, the same. That is to say, our DNA provides the plan for building a body, memories, instincts and so on. RNA provides the building blocks – in physical terms the amino acids – that make and sustain a body, and react to injury and sickness. It also, in ways we do not yet understand, provides the building blocks for our feelings (hormonal), moods (anger, passion, peace and so on), thoughts and memories.

The 64 I Ching readings provide insight into our situation at any given moment (the plan, as it were), and in their six degrees of change each provides us with the building blocks of the conduct of our lives. It is no surprise to me that there are so many exact correspondences between them, which I will now categorise.

Correspondence 1.

There are four nucleotide bases in DNA: Adenine (A), Thymine (T), Guanine (G) and Cytosine (C). These correspond in a way we will explore later to the four fundamental lines we may find in a hexagram: Stable yang (⸻), stable yin (▬ ▬), moving yang (▬⊖▬) and moving yin (▬✕▬). These can also be written as two-line symbols as ▬▬, ▬ ▬, ▬▬, and ▬ ▬ respectively.

Correspondence 2.

A always bonds with T using two hydrogen bonds.
G always bonds with C and the bond is made by three hydrogen bonds.

Three thousand years ago the sages who discovered, by trial and error, the principles of the I Ching, also used the numbers two and three as fundamental bonds. To quote the I Ching itself *"In ancient times the holy sages made the book of changes thus: They invented the yarrow-stalk oracle in order to lend aid in a mysterious way to the light of the gods. To heaven they assigned the number three and to earth they assigned the number two."* (*Wilhelm p262*). This 'co-incidence' has a deep resonance with the lines of the hexagram and their degrees of change.

Each line of a hexagram was and is generated by casting yarrow sticks three times or throwing three coins. They assigned to Head the number three, to Tail the number two. The total in three coins then are as follows:

TTT = 2+2+2 = 6 interpreted as moving yin. The probability is 1 in 8.

TTH, THT or HTT = 2+2+3 = 7 interpreted as stable yang. The probability is 3 in 8.

THH, HTH or HHT = 2+3+3 = 8 interpreted as stable yin. The probability is 3 in 8.

HHH = 3+3+3 = 9 interpreted as moving yang. The probability is 1 in 8.

(2 and 3 were also assigned to the results of drawing yarrow sticks, with virtually the same probabilities of totals 6,7,8 and 9).

A DNA 'swatch' consists of three pairs of bases, which will give a three-letter codon when unzipped and read as mRNA. The total number of hydrogen bonds in any three-pair swatch is 6,7,8 or 9 depending on the swatch. If all three pairs are A – T   (or of course T – A or any combination) the total number of hydrogen bonds is 6. There are 8 ways this can happen. (AT,AT,AT), (AT,AT,TA), (AT,TA,AT), (TA,AT,AT), (AT,TA,TA), (TA,AT,TA), (TA,TA,AT), and (TA,TA,TA).

If two pairs are A – T (or T – A) and one is G – C (or C – G) the total number of hydrogen bonds is 7. There are 24 ways this can happen. (Believe me or try it for yourself!)

If one pair is A – T (or T – A) and two are G – C (or C – G) the total number of hydrogen bonds is 8, and again there are 24 ways this can happen.

If all three pairs are G – C (or C – G) the total number of hydrogen bonds is 9. There are 8 ways this can happen.

That is, the probability of 6 Hydrogen bonds is 8 out of 64 = 1 in 8: of 7 Hydrogen bonds is 24 out of 64 = 3 in 8; of 8 bonds is also 24 out of 64 = 3 in 8; and of 9 bonds is 8 out of 64 = 1 in 8.

In other words, the probability of 6, 7, 8, or 9 hydrogen bonds is the same as the probability of a particular line being moving yin, stable yang, stable yin and moving yang, respectively.

Correspondence 3.

A DNA swatch consists of three paired bases. For instance, the

DNA swatch $\begin{bmatrix} 3 & T - A & 6 \\ 2 & G - C & 5 \\ 1 & C - G & 4 \end{bmatrix}$ has, (from the bottom), C paired with G (1 and 4); G paired with C (2 and 5) and T paired with A (3 and 6).

The same pairing was noted by the ancient sages in a hexagram, as we noted in chapter six. To quote James Legge in his *Translator's introduction to the I Ching*, "The lines, moreover, are related to one another by their position, and have their significance modified accordingly. The first line and the fourth, the second and the fifth, the third and the sixth, are all correlates, and to make the correlation perfect the two members of it should be lines of different qualities, one whole, one divided."(*op. cit. p16*)

Richard Wilhelm notes the same connection. "Lines occupying analogous places in the lower and upper trigram sometimes have an especially close relationship. As a rule, firm lines correspond with yielding lines only, and vice versa." *(op. cit. p361)*

Admittedly, we require correspondence whether the lines are opposites or not, but the subtlety of firm and yielding will not be lost. This pairing of line 1 with line 4, line 2 with line 5, and line 3 with line 6 is fundamental to the great correspondence (5, below), where each of the 64 different possible DNA swatches can be shown to correspond exactly to a particular hexagram of the 64 possibles.

Correspondence 4.

The four possibilities for each of the three pairs of lines of a hexagram, ▬▬▬, ▬ ▬, ▬▬▬, and ▬▬ ▬▬ split into two types: ▬▬▬ and ▬▬ ▬▬ are types of yang; while ▬ ▬ and ▬▬ ▬▬ are types of yin. The same is true of the four nucleotide bases: Adenine and Guanine are purines, double-ringed molecules; while Thymine and Cytosine are pyrimidines, single-ringed molecules.

Correspondence 5.

We are now in a position to note the most amazing correspondence of all: that the Old Family chart of all 64 hexagrams corresponds exactly with the DNA chart of all 64 possible swatches arranged in the groups which demonstrate which codons attract which amino acids. On the way we will stumble across Correspondence 6.

INTRODUCTION TO THIS ASTONISHING CORRESPONDENCE.

Let me begin by saying that what follows is complicated and requires at least an amateur understanding of the biology of DNA – the unique blueprint we each carry – and an appreciation of mathematical pattern and the equivalence of ideas. Because you may not wish to soldier through all the complexities, I shall begin with the conclusion. And what an amazing conclusion it is! It turns out that the pattern of the 64 Hexagrams which the Chinese philosophers reasoned out as being the key to understanding our own unconscious minds is exactly the same pattern as is found in the 64 codons table above. I say exactly because the table preserves the blocks of two, three, and four amino acids we noted in the table on page 111. It even preserves the split blocks of Serine, Leucine and Arginine.

You will recall that in chapter six (page 80) we introduced the 'Old Family' schematisation of the eight trigrams, where ☷ ☷ Earth was Mother; ☶ ☶ Mountain was 3rd daughter; ☵☵ Water was 2nd. daughter; ☴☴ Wood/wind was 1st daughter; ☳☳ Thunder was 1st son; ☲☲ Fire was 2nd son; ☱☱ Lake was 3rd son; and ☰ Heaven, was Father. The earliest written codification of the hexagrams generated by combining these trigrams was, according to Chinese legend, by Fu Hsi, some 5,000 years ago. How astonishing that he should have chosen the precise order that expresses the trigrams as binary numbers, from 0 to 7, as his order for the Old Family of trigrams. (If you imagine the symbols above turned through 90 degrees clockwise, you get ⚊⚊⚊; ⚊⚊, ⚊⚊, ⚊⚊, ⚊⚊, ⚊⚊, ⚊⚊, ⚊⚊⚊, which are the binary numbers 0,1,2,3,4,5,6,7 respectively.) To get the hexagrams in order, Fu Hsi wrote these trigrams across the top of a chart as the 'upper trigrams', then down the side of the chart as the 'lower trigrams', ending up with the chart below.

UPPER TRIGRAMS

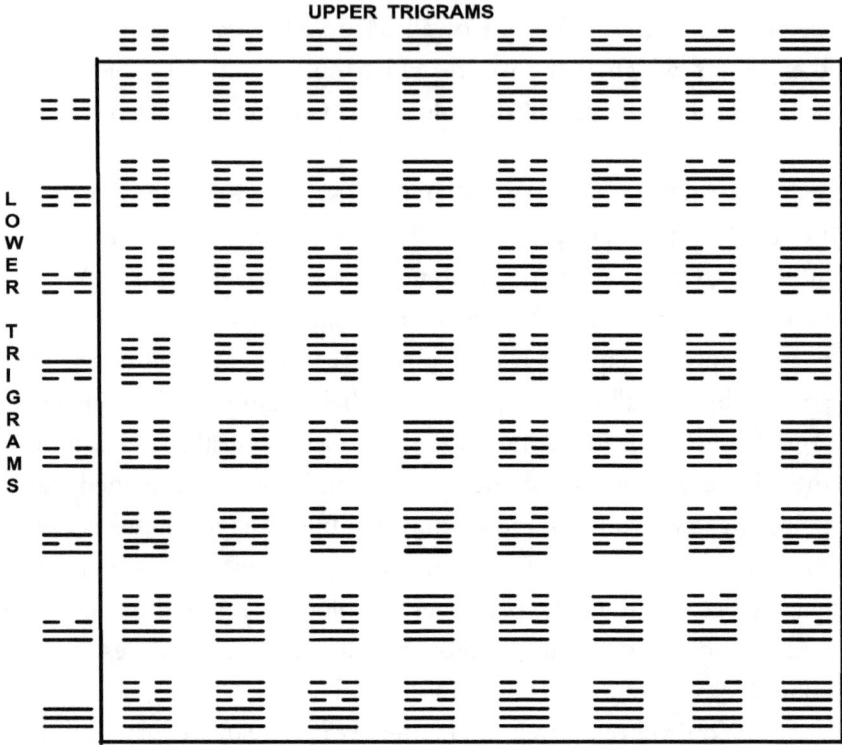

By turning each of these hexagrams through 90 degrees clockwise we get the binary numbers in rows reading the Arabic equivalent of 0 to 7 in the first line; 8 to 15 in the second; 16 to 23 in the third and so on to 56 to 63 on the bottom line. This was roughly 4,500 years before Leibnitz came up with the idea in the West, in 1679! But this is just the beginning. It further turns out that the natural grouping above accords with the grouping of the 20 amino acids and three stop signs which are made from the DNA plan in every living body: human, animal, plant, tree. The chart with the amino acids and stop/start signs included looks like this. (I have also included the three-letter codons which generate the amino acids, **written from the bottom up.**)

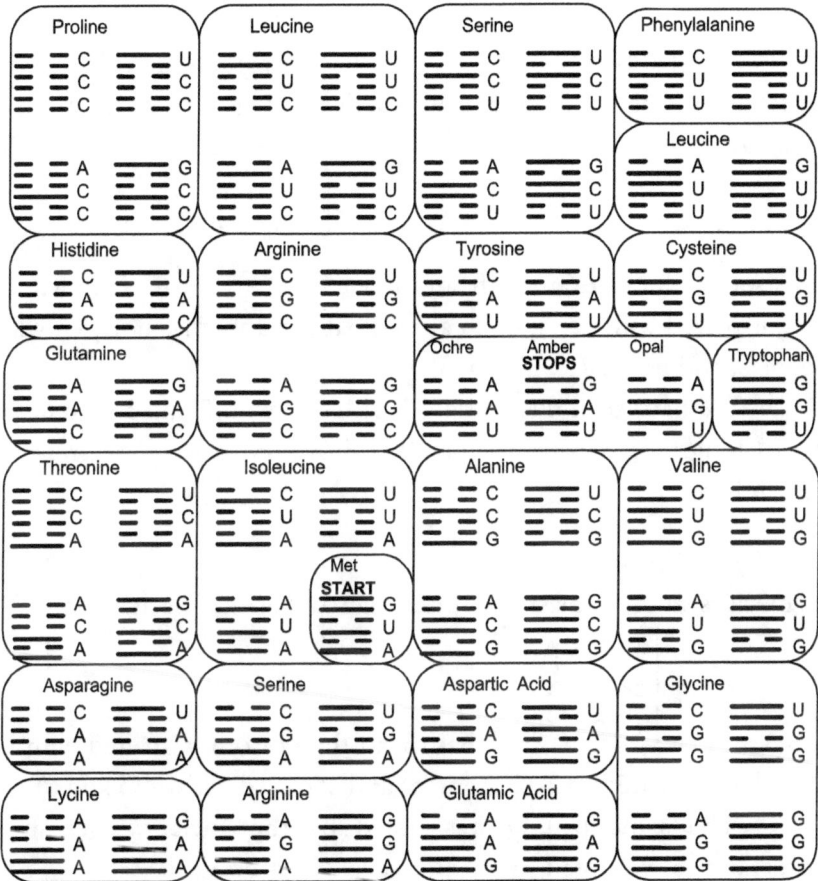

Proline	Leucine	Serine	Phenylalanine
C C C / U C C	C U C / U U C	C C U / U C U	C U U / U U U
A C C / G C C	A U C / G U C	A C U / G C U	**Leucine** A U U / G U U

Histidine	Arginine	Tyrosine	Cysteine
C A C / U A C	C G C / U G C	C A U / U A U	C G U / U G U

Glutamine	Ochre / Amber **STOPS** / Opal		Tryptophan
A A C / G A C	A A C / G A C	A A U / G A U	G G U / U G U

Threonine	Isoleucine	Alanine	Valine
C C A / U C A	C U A / U U A	C C G / U C G	C U G / U U G
A C A / G C A	**Met START** A U A / G U A	A C G / G C G	A U G / G U G

Asparagine	Serine	Aspartic Acid	Glycine
C A A / U A A	C G A / U G A	C A G / U A G	C G G / U G G

Lycine	Arginine	Glutamic Acid	
A A A / G A A	A G A / G G A	A A G / G A G	A G G / G G G

Let's be clear as to the enormity of this correspondence. The 5,000 year old fundamental 'Old Family' method of laying out the 64 hexagrams both gives the binary numbers in order from 0 to 63, and preserves the blocks of amino acids produced by the DNA plan. It would be no exaggeration simply to say **"The Old Family chart of the 64 I Ching hexagrams is the genetic code"**.

The mathematical and bio-chemical justification follows, for those prepared to take the journey.

WHICH HEXAGRAM SHOULD CORRESPOND TO WHICH DNA SWATCH?

We have established that there are 64 hexagrams and 64 DNA swatches. We need to find a logical way of generating a specific hexagram for a specific DNA swatch – set of three pairs of bases.

$$\begin{bmatrix} 3 & T - A & 6 \\ 2 & G - C & 5 \\ 1 & C - G & 4 \end{bmatrix}$$

Let's stay with our example from earlier, . Clearly, no. 1, C, is paired with no. 4, G, in a fixed pairing. Likewise no.2, G, with no. 5, C, and no. 3, T, with no. 6, A.

We have seen this pairing, 1 with 4, 2 with 5 and 3 with 6, in the I Ching too, as correspondence 3 above. For ease of reference I copy it here.

Correspondence 3
A DNA swatch consists of three paired bases. For instance, the

$$\begin{bmatrix} 3 & T - A & 6 \\ 2 & G - C & 5 \\ 1 & C - G & 4 \end{bmatrix}$$

DNA swatch has,(from the bottom) C paired with G (1 and 4); G paired with C (2 and 5) and T paired with A (3 and 6).

The same pairing was noted by the ancient sages in a hexagram, as we noted in chapter seven. To quote James Legge in his Translator's introduction to the I Ching, *"The lines, moreover, are related to one another by their position, and have their significance modified accordingly. The first line and the fourth, the second and the fifth, the third and the sixth, are all correlates, and to make the correlation perfect the two members of it should be lines of different qualities, one whole, one divided." (op. cit. p16)*

Richard Wilhelm notes the same connection. *"Lines occupying analogous places in the lower and upper trigram sometimes have an especially close relationship. As a rule, firm lines correspond with yielding lines only, and vice versa." (op. cit. p361)*

Admittedly, we require correspondence whether the lines are opposites or not, but the subtlety of firm and yielding will not be lost. This pairing of line 1 with line 4, line 2 with line 5, and line 3 with line 6 is fundamental to seeing the great correspondence, where each of the 64 different possible DNA swatches can be shown to correspond exactly to a particular hexagram of the 64 possibles.

There are four possible pairings in the I Ching. [symbol]; [symbol]; [symbol] and [symbol].

(Where the dot between the lines reminds us the top line will be in the upper trigram, the bottom line in the lower trigram.) The first is a firm line —— paired with a yielding — — and the second vice versa: what Legge (above) calls a perfect correlate. The third and fourth pair like with like and so are by definition 'imperfect', but we will use them nevertheless. We are going to equate these I Ching pairings to the four possible DNA base pairings, which are T – A, A – T, C – G and G – C, three of which appear in our example swatch above.

Which I Ching pairing shall we assign to which DNA pairing?

You will recall that A and G are double-ringed purines, and it is a fact that they each have 9 'nodes' where other molecules could attach. T and C are pyrimidines, single-ringed, with just 6 nodes available. Remember that 9 is the sages' number for moving yang, and 6 for moving yin: add in that the purines with their double-rings simply 'feel' like yang, while the pyrimidines with their single rings 'feel' more like yin, and I am ready to plump for the yin symbols to correlate to the pairings starting T and C, and the yang symbols to the pairings starting A and G. That means T – A corresponds either to [symbol] or [symbol], C – G to the other (these are stable and moving yin). Likewise A – T corresponds to [symbol] or [symbol] and G – C to the other. It seems reasonable that [symbol] is the opposite to [symbol], and [symbol] the opposite to [symbol]. Beyond that it doesn't matter which way we choose: we just get perfectly acceptable mirror images in the final chart. In order to produce what is now accepted as the Standard Chart, we will pick as follows, and make it the rule.

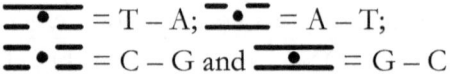

$$\equiv\!\bullet\!\equiv = T - A; \quad \overline{\equiv\!\bullet\!\equiv} = A - T;$$
$$\equiv\!\bullet\!\equiv = C - G \text{ and } \underline{\equiv\!\bullet\!\equiv} = G - C$$

Let's apply this to our example DNA swatch,
$$\begin{bmatrix} 3 & \text{T - A} & 6 \\ 2 & \text{G - C} & 5 \\ 1 & \text{C - G} & 4 \end{bmatrix}.$$

Writing up from the bottom, as always in I Ching, C – G gives $\equiv\!\bullet\!\equiv$, i.e. __ __ as line 1 and __ __ as line 4. G – C gives _____ as line 2 and _____ as line 5. Finally T – A gives __ __ as line 3 and _____ as line 6. Putting these together gives the hexagram

, No. 59 Dispersion (Dissolving of blocks).

Obviously we could make the correspondence the other way too, for instance (Hexagram 40, Deliverance) corresponds to bottom line T – A, next line A – T and top line C – G: the swatch
$$\begin{bmatrix} \text{C - G} \\ \text{A - T} \\ \text{T - A} \end{bmatrix}.$$ Putting all the corresponding hexagrams in the Old Family chart, which you will remember is also the binary numbers from 0 to 63, we get the chart shown opposite.

Notes:

1) I have put the 'left' side of each DNA swatch beside each corresponding hexagram, written as it was in the original swatch – from the bottom upwards, but writing T as U, as in the unzipping process Thymine becomes Uracil. (Our CGT becomes CGU and is there in row 3 column 4, and produces arginine eventually).

2) To read these as the normal codons in a book of bio-chemistry remember we are reading from the bottom up. e.g.

U
G
C

becomes the codon CGU.

Proline	Leucine	Serine	Phenylalanine
C U	C U	C U	C U
C C	U U	C C	U U
C C	C C	U U	U U
			Leucine
A G	A G	A G	A G
C C	U U	C C	U U
C C	C C	U U	U U
Histidine	**Arginine**	**Tyrosine**	**Cysteine**
C U	C U	C U	C U
A A	G G	A A	G G
C C	C C	U U	U U
Glutamine		Ochre Amber **STOPS**	Opal Tryptophan
A G	A G	A G	A G
A A	G G	A A	G G
C C	C C	U U	U U
Threonine	**Isoleucine**	**Alanine**	**Valine**
C U	C U	C U	C U
C C	U U	C C	U U
A A	A A	G G	G G
	Met **START**		
A G	A G	A G	A G
C C	U U	C C	U U
A A	A A	G G	G G
Asparagine	**Serine**	**Aspartic Acid**	**Glycine**
C U	C U	C U	C U
A A	G G	A A	G G
A A	A A	G G	G G
Lycine	**Arginine**	**Glutamic Acid**	
A G	A G	A G	A G
A A	G G	A A	G G
A A	A A	G G	G G

To recognise the astonishing significance of this, just realise that any other chart of the hexagrams would have produced a random splattering of each of the amino acids, yet here we have them in exactly the same blocks as they appear in bio-chemical charts, even down to the split four and two in the cases of Serine, Leucine and Arginine. The 'Stop' codons are together. The one simple pattern of the binary numbers 0 to 63 ties the I Ching hexagrams and the DNA codons together.

Remember too the five correspondences we noted and used in order to find the rule that assigned particular hexagrams to particular DNA swatches.

1) There are four elements in each system – the nucleotides in DNA and the four possible lines, stable yang (———), stable yin (— —), moving yang (—⊖—) and moving yin (—✕—) in the I Ching.

2) The number of hydrogen bonds in a DNA swatch, and their exact parallel to the numbers assigned 5,000 years ago to the four I Ching possible lines. And the fact that the probabilities of 6,7,8 or 9 hydrogen bonds in the swatch are exactly the same as the probabilities of a total of 6,7,8 or 9 in the throwing of three coins.

3) The fact that in a numbered swatch 1 & 4; 2 & 5; 3 & 6 are paired irrevocably, while the ancient sages also posited a similar, though less definite, pairing in a hexagram.

4) The four possible hexagram lines split into two pairs (yang types and yin types): the nucleotides also split into two purines and two pyrimidines.

5) The sixth line in a hexagram was understood to be different in character from the other five, in that it was 'less involved' or 'more ethereal' than they are. Nucleotide 6 in a swatch specifies the third nucleotide in a codon, and this generally makes no difference to the amino acid produced. For instance, CGU,CGC,CGA and CGG all produce Arginine. This is the sixth correspondence I promised we would stumble on.

It is no exaggeration to say in terms of mathematical patterning, the Old Family chart of the I Ching hexagrams **is identical to** the bio-chemical chart of codons and amino acids. And that **both are identical** to the 8 x 8 layout of the binary numbers 0 to 63. This identity suggests to me the possibility (no more, but no less) that the I Ching may work in the same way as our DNA does. That is to say that just as our DNA is being continually unzipped and read to produce amino acids which combine to form the proteins that keep our physical bodies healthy and renewed, so regular recourse to the I Ching readings gives a valuable ongoing insight into our unconscious which serves to keep our psyche healthy and supple. To those who dismiss out-of-hand the notion that tossing coins or separating yarrow sticks could possibly unlock such an insight, please see chapters ten and eleven on Synchronicity and Entanglement.

There is a further correspondence to be found, now we have the identical chart for the binary numbers, the bio-chemical codons and the I Ching hexagrams. We note that amino acids are produced in blocks: that is, for instance, Proline is produced by the block CCC, CCU, CCA and CCG. It is also the case that the four hexagrams in that block produce readings with a common theme, as shown below.

Proline: equivalent to hexagrams nos. 2, 23, 15 & 52.

2: The Receptive.

Yielding and devoted. Image of the mare. Consistent seriousness.

23. Splitting apart (Disintegration).

This is a condition of the times – bad things happen. The right behaviour in such times is inner docility and devotion, and outward stillness. Although usually unpleasant, times of disintegration are a necessary part of things and should be seen as precursors to better times.

15. Modesty.

Moderation in all things. Men hate arrogance, and love modesty.

52. Keeping still.

Reacting appropriately to the demands of the time. There is a time to keep still, quiet, calm, and if this is one of them, take notice! We need to be very aware of our inner state in order to achieve this stillness, but it is worth the effort.

Common theme: Acceptance of one's lot – not 'kicking against the pricks'.

In fact, just as each amino acid is produced by several codons in a block, so the equivalent blocks produce groups of hexagrams also sharing a common theme. It would be disruptive here to repeat the process in all 24 blocks, so this is done, for the sake of completeness, in Part Two. (Chapters 12 – 14).

Again, let's acknowledge the significance of what we have here. Not only do the Hexagrams and DNA codons conform to the same fundamental pattern as the binary number 8 x 8 matrix, but the blocks of readings where several codons produce the same amino acid show the same homogeneity of I Ching readings produced. The fundamentals of each of the readings in a block is the same – they apply to similar circumstances. To put it another way each hexagram in a block is engaging the same archetype, or groups of archetypes – in my terminology, accessing the same unknown knowns.

Chapter eight

God invented the counting numbers...

THE SIGNIFICANCE OF THE IDENTICAL PATTERNS:
BINARY NUMBERS, DNA CODONS AND I CHING HEXAGRAMS.

What might Pauli, the great physicist and mathematician, have made of these identical patterns? How might Jung have reacted to the discovery that the DNA which carries every generation's physical characteristics to the next generation shares its pattern with the ancient Chinese oracle he so admired? Sadly the discovery came after each was dead.

This far we have been on solid ground. The history and friendship of Jung and Pauli are well-documented; Jung's theory of synchronicity (see chapter ten) is as well-expressed as it can be; the bizarre nature of quantum mechanics is accepted as true; and the correspondence between the patterns of the binary numbers, the DNA codons and the I Ching hexagrams demonstrated.

Unsure of quite where to go from here I took my own advice and consulted the I Ching, with the question "What is it that I'm really trying to deduce from these amazing correspondences?" The answer was ☷, Number 46, changing on line 2 and line 5. This reading is entitled Pushing Upward, with the image of a plant or seed growing within the earth. (An obvious picture, as the hexagram is made up of Wood below Earth.) I quote from the reading itself:

THE CONDITION

The picture of wood growing within the earth gives the idea of pushing upward. In contrast with Easy Progress (no. 35) where the sun rising over the earth indicates easy expansion, Pushing Upward is associated with effort, as a plant, needing energy to maintain growth.

THE JUDGEMENT

> *Pushing upward has supreme success.*
> *One should seek great men: seek advice,*
> *And set to work; for activity is favoured.*

The gentle is within (Wood); devotion is without (Earth). Pushing upward is made possible not by violence, but by modesty and adaptability. The reason for success is not an earthly but a transcendental one. The favourableness of conditions comes from the invisible world. We should make the most of the time, whilst we can, through work.

THE IMAGE

> *As wood grows within the earth*
> *So the wise man, of devoted character,*
> *Heaps up small things*
> *To achieve something high and great.*

To understand how a tree is contracted into a seed is to understand the future unfolding of the seed into a tree. To know this movement is to know the future.

I have emboldened the sentence above because it leapt out at me as specifying the way forward, though of course I found the whole reading very comforting at this stage of my exploration. Likewise, the two changing lines bring comfort at this critical moment, moving from the known into the unknown. They run:

> Line 2: *If one is sincere and upright*
> *One should bring even a small offering.*

I acknowledge that from here on I am on tentative ground: I offer my thoughts for others to ponder and work with. (As the Judgement says: *One should seek great men: seek advice.*)

What follows are amateur ideas without the bio-chemistry to back them up.

> Line 5: *Pushing upward by steps. Persevere.*

This is amplified thus: When advancing it is important not to become intoxicated by success. Go slowly, step by step, as if hesitant. Only calm, steady progress leads to the goal.

'TO UNDERSTAND HOW A TREE IS CONTRACTED INTO A SEED IS TO UNDERSTAND THE FUTURE UNFOLDING OF THE SEED INTO A TREE.'

With the discovery of DNA we do now understand how a tree is contracted into a seed, and how the seed unfolds into a tree. The bio-chemistry of a DNA chromosome as a tightly packed and complete blueprint for reproduction is well understood, as is its continuous unzipping into codons to produce amino acids, and hence proteins, for growth. The critical step I need to take is to extend this understanding to the human unconscious mind. It is clear that our unconscious (and of course our conscious) mind rests in a physical place, within our brain. It is not some metaphysical concept, but a physical entity, and one might expect it to be located in the oldest part of our brain, the 'reptilian' brainstem and cerebellum. This however is concerned only with our involuntary actions – breathing, heartbeat and so on – whereas the next layer up, the 'limbic', is a much more likely candidate. The limbic brain emerged in the first mammals and its main structures are the hippocampus, the amygdala, and the hypothalamus. The limbic brain is the seat of the value judgments that we make, often unconsciously, that exert such a strong influence on our behaviour. Here, surely, is the seat of our unknown knowns, the collective archetypes and the 'personal unconscious' – the accretion of forgotten experiences that still influence our actions and personality.

Since this limbic brain is a physical reality, it must be transmitted first to the seed as part of the DNA chromosomes, and then, as the person grows, be fed from the unzipped DNA via amino acids in the same way as all other cells in the body. If Jung is correct in his theory that the archetypes of the collective unconscious are universal then they must also be transmitted in our DNA, in some

127

part that is common to everyone – presumably the mitochondrial. Mitochondrial DNA is passed entirely through mothers, and is the same chromosome in all humans, leading to the theory that we are all descended from 'Mitochondrial Eve' – a female Homo Sapiens living in Africa somewhere between 100,000 to 200,000 years ago. Certainly, from their discovery in the early 1800s until the mid-1950s mitochondria were commonly believed to transmit hereditary information.

It may be hard to accept that apparently abstract concepts such as the various archetypes – the anima, the shadow, the trickster and so on – could be encoded in DNA and so inherited, but there are many other abstractions which surely must be. Think for a moment of the range of instinctive behaviour in all animals that is certainly not learnt. Sea turtles, newly hatched on a beach, will automatically move toward the ocean. A joey kangaroo climbs into its mother's pouch upon being born. Honeybees communicate by dancing in the direction of a food source without formal instruction. Other examples include animal fighting, animal courtship behaviour, the building of nests and the migratory routes taken, particularly by solitary birds such as ospreys, at the end of their first summer. These instincts must be embedded in some aspect of inherited DNA, just as surely as more normal physical attributes.

We may then have at least an overview of how our collective unconscious, all those archetypes, those unknown knowns, are 'contracted into a seed' – even if we have no bio-chemical knowledge of the actual mechanism. How might the seed 'unfold into the tree'? In other words, how might we access this unconscious knowledge lurking in our limbic brains? Here my knowledge is even sketchier, and I can only 'heap up the small things' spoken of in the image of 'Pushing Upward' above. Pauli and Jung wrestled for a quarter of a century with the question "What is the physics of psychology?" without achieving any definite answers. Our only advantage is the discovery and mapping of DNA and the insights into amino acid production. Here are my small heaps:

Heap 1.

In common with all other cells in our bodies, those in our limbic brains contain DNA which is constantly unzipping and being read. These are the cells wherein our unknown knowns lurk. Might their possible release to our conscious brain be to do with this process of unzipping?

Heap 2.

We have seen that the ancient hexagrams of the I Ching are mathematically identical in pattern to that of the codons, when set out in the, arguably, simplest way: that is as an 8 x 8 table of the binary counting numbers 0 to 63. Might it be that the ribosomes reading these particular codons are producing something for the production of archetypes, as well as proteins? We know there are huge tranches of mRNA which are not involved in amino acid production; perhaps some of these are being read in a different fashion to maintain the archetypes in the limbic brain.

Heap 3.

Since the hexagrams have the same pattern as the codons, is it possible that any particular codon being produced in the limbic brain is, in a quantum mechanics fashion, 'entangled' with its matching hexagram? If it were, might any observation made of it – which might be the spinning of coins or collecting of yarrow sticks – inevitably affect the hexagram too? For a fuller exposition, see chapter eleven.

I do realise these are merely kites I am flying, easily dismissible as flights of fancy, but I take a little comfort from the speculations of Erasmus Darwin, grandfather of Charles, at the end of the eighteenth century. We are, perhaps, at the same stage in our lack of understanding of the workings of our unconscious as he was about our DNA, when the best he could manage was that there were 'living filaments' in common between animals and vegetables. Nevertheless, his illustrious grandson was able to make great strides and begin our understanding of evolution, and the discovery of DNA vindicated his meditations completely.

Here's a long quotation from Erasmus Darwin's seminal work *Zoonomia; or the laws of organic life*, published in 1795, nearly 160 years before Watson and Crick.

"From thus meditating on the great similarity of the structure of the warm-blooded animals, and at the same time of the great changes they undergo both before and after their nativity; and by considering in how minute a proportion of time many of the changes of animals above described have been produced; would it be too bold to imagine, that in the great length of time, since the earth began to exist, perhaps millions of years...that **all warm-blooded animals have arisen from one living filament, which THE GREAT FIRST CAUSE endued with animality...and thus possessing the faculty of continuing to improve by its own inherent activity, and of delivering down those improvements by generation to its posterity, world without end?"** (My emphasis).

"Shall we then say that the vegetable living filament was originally different from that of each tribe of animals above described? And that the productive living filament of each of those tribes was different originally from the other? Or, as the earth and ocean were probably peopled with vegetable productions long before the existence of animals...**shall we conjecture that one and the same kind of living filament is and has been the cause of all organic life?"** (My emphasis).

In the same way I am suggesting that Jung's 'collective unconscious' requires living filaments, common to us all, and that as with Erasmus Darwin's filaments, these too are DNA.

SECULARISM AND ATHEISM
If these archetypes lurk in our subconscious, ready to project onto other people or situations, and we have no religion to give them any form in our conscious minds – what then? We have seen, in this last century, two great experiments in atheistic secularism – and neither

gives any grounds for its recommendation. The USSR under Joseph Stalin and communist China under Mao Tse-tung both attempted to remove religion and both achieved the mass starvation and brutalisation of huge swathes of their populations. With the suppression of the more 'spiritual', or at least altruistic of our archetypes came the vaunting of the more unpleasant archetypes: the Trickster, the cruder Yang figures, the Warrior and so on. It is arguable that communism itself, if enforced and not altruistic, is an archetype which can only flourish under a dictatorship – an archetype of the bully, the savage and the manipulator.

Nevertheless, the Western world has drifted well down the stream of atheism and secularism. Church attendance in general is at an all-time low, and still sinking. Disgust at the terrorism and bigotry of fundamental Islam drains away respect for all religion – as indeed does the recognition that Christianity in its youth and middle age was every bit as repugnant. Sophisticated Westerners can no longer believe in the old myths – heaven and hell, life after death, a God way above the skies, creation in 4004 BC – but cannot find new metaphors for the spiritual life struggling for existence in their hearts. Or, more accurately, for the unknown knowns swarming in their limbic brains.

What can be done? How can we find a spirituality for our times? Finding no answer in my own heart, I once again turned to the I Ching itself, with the question "What can be done about the demise

of religion in the West?" The answer was ☰☵, Reading no. 47, Oppression, changing on line one. It is worth looking at all aspects of the reading:

THE CONDITION

The hexagram depicts a lake that is empty. It is dried up, exhausted, because an abyss has opened up within it and beneath it.

When there is no water in the lake conditions are exceptional. It represents a time when superior men, everywhere, are oppressed and held in restraint by inferior men. Certainly a very good description of the state I was describing!

THE JUDGEMENT

> *Oppression is a test of character:*
> *It leads to perplexity and thence to success.*
> *When one has something to say*
> *One gets no hearing; one is not believed.*
> *But through oppression does one learn*
> *To lessen one's rancour.*

Does this help us at all? At the moment we are at the 'perplexity' stage… let's hope we can make it through to success. At all events, it is no help just to rant and rave about the situation.

THE IMAGE

> *The lake is dried up, exhausted.*
> *When adverse fate befalls him*
> *The wise man stakes his life on following his will.*

Here then is advice, if we can find a way of following it. My personal will is to contact my unknown knowns in every situation, but how might this aid the Western world out of its increasing state of all-too-conscious secularism? Let's turn to the moving line (line one) and read its degree of change.

> *One sits oppressed under a bare tree;*
> *One strays into a gloomy valley.*

I read this as an admonition to move away from 'the bare tree', and out of 'the gloomy valley'. The bare tree, for those for whom Christianity has lost its appeal, is the traditional picture of Christianity. It was, once, fully leafed, and sheltered those who came to it. It did, once, bear great fruit, spiritual blessing for its followers and all that they did in its name. But now it is bare; unable to provide either shade or fruit. There is of course another metaphor here for Christians: the bare tree can be seen as the cross. Obviously not intended by the Taoist sages, but we bring our own cultures to our

132

readings of the I Ching. Some of us are indeed oppressed by the cross and all its overwhelming weight of symbolism – sacrifice, atonement, grace overcoming our original sin. For many people in the West, these are tired metaphors which no longer provide inspiration or comfort.

The gloomy valley inevitably conjures a vision of the 'valley of the shadow of death'. We are to move away from this valley, this unhelpful preoccupation with death and some sort of eternal life. We have forgotten the more optimistic and life-affirming sayings attributed to Jesus in the gospels: 'I come that you may have life, and have it in all its fullness' *(John 10:10)*.

This thought leads me on to another aspect of the I Ching; one that I have rather neglected both in my own life and in this book. There is a school of thought that says one should look not only at the original hexagram and the degrees of change that may have been indicated, but also at the hexagram it is changing into. That is, the hexagram it becomes when the changing line has completely changed. In our case here ䷹ moves on to ䷹, reading no. 58, The Joyous! Here are its attributes:

THE CONDITION
The Joyous is symbolised by the smiling lake which refreshes and rejoices all life. True joy rests on firmness and strength within, manifesting itself outwardly as yielding and gentle.

THE JUDGEMENT
> *The joyous succeeds through steadfastness;*
> *For, if one is both joyous and steadfast,*
> *One accords with both God and man.*

THE IMAGE
> *As two lakes join to replenish each other,*
> *So the wise man joins with his friends*
> *To discuss and practise the truths of life.*

Putting the two readings and the degree of change together, it seems that the I Ching's answer to the question "What can be done about the demise of religion in the West?" is that we need to recognise that, for many, unreformed Christianity has had its day in our culture, though it prospers in many less developed countries. It is a bare tree offering neither shelter nor sustenance. Nevertheless, the archetypes in our collective unconscious demand recognition. They demand recognition on the individual level, or we remain two-dimensional cardboard cut-outs; and they demand recognition at group levels, or they will manifest as mob violence, religious persecution, terrorism and outright war. I find regular consultation of the I Ching satisfies my individual need for in-dividuation, but group exploration needs, as it has always needed, religious outlet – a church of some kind. In a scientific, rational world it is difficult to envisage what sort of church this might be, but the readings above suggest it should be based on joyfulness. And yet, because it must reflect all the swirling archetypes that bind us together it must be able to comprehend and take the sting from jealousy, envy, sexual frenzy, warped mother fixations, territorialism, anger…. all those negative archetypes which so often engulf a group and end in violence and bloodshed. It must, somehow, reveal to us our unknown knowns.

Part two

In Part One I was anxious to move the argument on as efficiently as possible in order not to disrupt the flow unnecessarily. Here in Part Two we look at some of the side issues which are fascinating in themselves, and indeed have a bearing on the hypothesis that the codons of our mRNA and the readings of the I Ching, when laid out as binary numbers display a meaningful correspondence.

Firstly we look at the various methods of consulting the I Ching, and find that even there the idea of Quaternity over Trinity plays a cameo role. We then move on to have a longer look at Jung's thesis that what he called Synchronicity is a reality in everyone's life. That is, that sometimes two events happen which can have no causal effect on each other, but which nevertheless are found to have a meaningful relationship to each other. Usually, but not necessarily, one of these is a psychic event – that is a thought, a dream or a strong feeling, and the other is a physical event clearly related to the first, but with no apparent causation between them.

We move on then to look at the complex Quantum Physics concept of Entanglement, which is gaining ground as a possible conduit for synchronicity. Here we are very much in the realm of hypothesis and conjecture, but it is worth, even from an amateur point of view, looking at some of the recent conjectures, especially as they actually bring us full circle to the Jungian thesis of the collective unconscious which was the original springboard for this book.

Lastly there are a couple of chapters hazarding the conjecture that the hexagrams corresponding to blocks of codons producing the same amino acid are themselves related, in a similar fashion.

Chapter nine

Methods of consulting the I Ching.

Three coins.

The simplest method, as mentioned several times in previous chapters, is to throw three coins to generate each line of the hexagram, working from the bottom up. So in total you throw 18 coins, in six groups of three. If you want to approach it as the Chinese, you give a head the value 3, and a tail the value 2, and use the rule we visited in chapter seven as correspondence 2. That is: Total 6 = moving yin; total 7 = yang; total 8 = yin; total 9 = moving yang. More simply, 3 tails = moving yin; 1 head, 2 tails = yang; 1 tail, 2 heads = yin; 3 heads = moving yang. (It is odd, but of a piece with the whole philosophy, that just one head with two tails gives yang.)

For a while you'll need to draw the results from the bottom up to see which hexagram is formed. For instance, if the first throw gives 1 H 2 T, draw ――― as the bottom line. If the next is 2 H 1 T, add ― ― above it. If the next is 3 T draw ―✕― as line three. 2 T 1H adds ――― as line 4, then say 3 H gives ―⊖― as line 5, and maybe 1 T 2 H gives ― ― as line 6. Putting these all together gives

⚎ which you look up in a book or online to find is No. 17, Following, with degrees of change 3 and 5 indicated.

It's a good idea to recognise the hexagram from the beginning as 'Lake over Thunder', since the top trigram is a version of ☱, and the bottom trigram is ☳. This helps to learn what you are doing each time.

I find it better to throw the three coins one after the other, rather than all together. I think it gives time for our unconscious to recognise what is happening: and it mirrors the yarrow stick method.

The yarrow stick method of generating lines.

Yarrow is a woody plant which can easily be cut to give sticks of equal length and diameter. In practice, we would now use Spillikins. Fifty sticks are used, in the following way.

Firstly, one is discarded, to leave 49, which are split at random into two piles – a right and a left hand pile. One stick is taken from the right hand pile and placed between the ring and little finger of the right hand.

Then the left hand heap is counted off in fours till four or fewer sticks are left. These are placed between the middle and ring finger of the right hand.

This is repeated on the right hand pile, and the remainder placed between the index and middle finger.

There will be found to be either 5 or 9 sticks held in the right hand. (We'll look at the Maths later). If there are 5, a score of 3 is entered: if 9, a score of 2, in the same way as using coins a head scores 3, a tail scores 2.

These 5 or 9 sticks are discarded and the remaining 44 or 40 sticks are gathered together and split again into a left and a right hand heap. The same procedure is gone through. This time there are again two possible results. There will be 1 stick between ring and little finger, and either 2 between middle and ring and 1 between index and middle, or 3 between middle and ring and 4 between index and middle. (Again, Maths later). These give a total of either 4 or 8. If there are 4, a score of 3 is entered; if there are 8, a score of 2 is entered.

These 4 or 8 are then also discarded, leaving a pile of either 40, 36, or 32 sticks. The procedure is undertaken again, and the results will once again be 4 or 8 sticks between the fingers of the right hand. Again, 4 is given a score of 3, 8 of 2.

These three scores are then totalled, as either 3+3+3=9, 3+3+2=8, 3+2+3=8, 3+2+2=7, 2+3+3=8, 2+3+2=7 or 2+2+2=6, and the convention we saw in chapter seven is that 9 signifies moving yang, 8 signifies yin, 7 signifies yang and 6 signifies moving yin. Thus is the first (bottom) line of the hexagram established.

This entire procedure is then gone through a further five times to build up the hexagram from the bottom upwards.

This is quite time-consuming, but I have come to think that is partly the point. You are concentrating on the mechanics, and your unconscious has a chance to influence how you split your heap each time. It turns out that the likelihood of moving yang is 3 in 16, of moving yin is 1 in 16, of fixed yang is 5 in 16 and of fixed yin is 7 in 16. This is not quite the same as is obtained by spinning coins: here moving yang is three times more likely than moving yin, whereas with coins they are the same. This slight lop-sidedness is typical of the Eastern tradition, while the strict symmetry of the coins is more Western.

Does it matter? Well, James Legge only considers the yarrow sticks – and then in scathing disbelief of any possible divination powers *(I Ching, book of changes,1996 edition, p 42)*. Wilhelm describes both methods, without discerning any difference in probabilities *(op. cit. p721-724)*, and in his preface Jung also accepts both methods, without prejudice to either. I will leave my own answer till we have looked at the quite complex Maths of the yarrow stalk method.

The Maths

We start with the 49 sticks, reduced to 48 by the removal of one to the right hand (between ring and little finger). When split into two heaps there are three possibilities of interest to us.

a)Each is even, and each is divisible by 4 (e.g. 16 & 32; 12 & 36).

b) Each is even, but neither is divisible by 4 (e.g. 18 & 30; 14 & 34).

c) Each is odd.

In the case of (a) the remainder will be 4 in each case, giving a total of 9 between the fingers.

In (b), the remainder will be 2 in each case, giving a total of 5 between the fingers.

(c) is more complicated, and is really two different scenarios. If the right heap is of the form 4n+1, where n is an integer (e.g. 33=4x8+1) then its remainder will be 1. But the left hand heap will then necessarily be of the form 4n+3 (e.g. 15=4x3+3 if the right heap was 33), and its remainder will be 3. Total sticks in fingers in both cases is 5. The other scenario reverses right and left, still giving a total of 5.

Each of (a), (b) (ci) and (cii) is equally likely, so three results give a total of 5, only one gives a total of 9.

If you want an alternative confirmation, we can specify all the possible left and right hand heaps in pairs: (1:47), (2:46), (3:45), (4:44), (5:43) and so on. They are respectively type cii, b, ci, a, cii,...throughout, and only the (a) type give a total of 9.

That is the first draw of three for each line. The second draw starts with 44 sticks if the first total was 5, 40 if the first total was 9. These will behave identically because both are divisible by 4. When one stick is removed and put between ring and little finger of the right hand, either 43 or 39 sticks are left. Consider the 43: when split into two heaps, one will be even, one odd, and they will either be of the form 4n and 4m+3, where n and m are integers (e.g. 12 = 4x3; 31=4x7+3) or 4n+2 and 4m+1 (e.g. 22=4x5+2; 21=4x5+1). In the first case the number of sticks in the hand will be 8 (1+4+3), in the second it will be 4 (1+2+1). Each is equally likely. The same is true for 39, as the form of the two heaps is the same.

The third draw will start with either 43 less 4 or 8, = 39 or 35 sticks, or 39 less 4 or 8 = 35 or 31 sticks. Each of these totals will give the same result as draw two, since 31,35,and 39 are all of the form 4n+3, as was the case in draw two. That is to say, the third draw will also leave 4 or 8 sticks in the fingers, each equally likely.

So, we give scores of 3 for a five on the first draw, 2 for a nine: 3 for a four on the second draw and 2 for an eight; 3 for a four on the third draw and 2 for an eight. Pictorially, this can be represented as:

First draw	Second draw	Third draw	Total score
	4	4	9
5		8	8
	8	4	8
		8	7
	4	4	9
5		8	8
	8	4	8
		8	7
	4	4	9
5		8	8
	8	4	8
		8	7
	4	4	8
9		8	7
	8	4	7
		8	6

And from this, simply counting the total scores, we see

Probability of a 9 is 3 in 16 (that is of a moving yang)

Probability of an 8 is 7 in 16 (yin)

Probability of a 7 is 5 in 16 (yang)

Probability of a 6 is 1 in 16 (moving yin)

The equivalent probabilities when spinning three coins are:

2 in 16 for moving yang

6 in 16 for yin

6 in 16 for yang

2 in 16 for moving yin.

So, spinning coins reduces the probability of a moving yin by a half, and increases the probability of a moving yang by a half.

The Quaternity of coins

It is clear that the Chinese sages intended this skewing of probabilities, because they could have produced the symmetry of the three-coin tossing method simply by starting with 48 yarrow sticks. Then the only numbers of sticks collected in the fingers would have been 4 or 8 on each draw, with the same probability for each. But they chose 49, and so deliberately skewed the probabilities of moving yang to 3 in 16, and of moving yin to 1 in 16, (And, in compensation, of fixed yang to 5 in 16 and of fixed yin to 7 in 16.)

It is in fact easy to replicate this result using coins. All we need to do is to follow the Chinese pattern and find a way of making the first spun coin three times more likely to be head than tail. This is easy – we simply spin two coins for the first result and say if there are any heads it counts as a head. There are four possible results HH, HT, TH, TT and three of the four show a head. The next two coins are thrown in the ordinary fashion. I am delighted by this simple solution, as it mirrors Pauli's fourth particle, the neutrino, which turned out to be needed in order to make an atom stable, and of course also fits perfectly with Jung's observation that four, not three, is the archetypal number, and the Quaternity far preferable to the Trinity.

The pattern is shown below, for clarity's sake. Remember the rule on the first spin of two coins is that it counts as a Head if any Head appears and a Tail only if no Head appears.

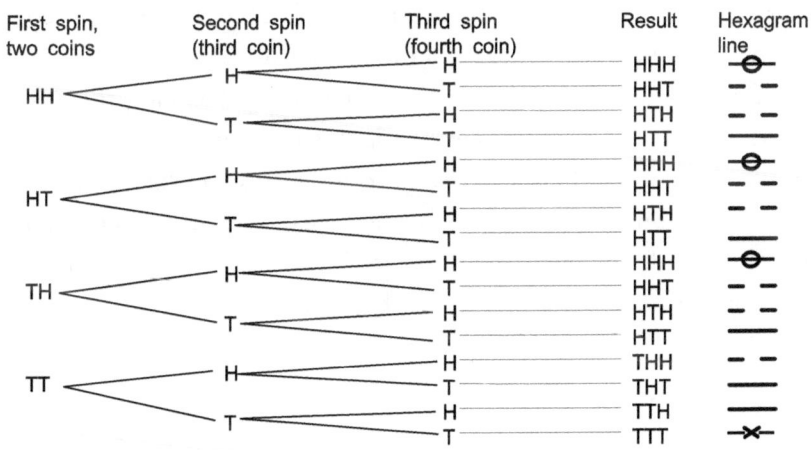

First spin, two coins	Second spin (third coin)	Third spin (fourth coin)	Result	Hexagram line
HH	H	H	HHH	—⊖—
		T	HHT	— —
	T	H	HTH	— —
		T	HTT	———
HT	H	H	HHH	—⊖—
		T	HHT	— —
	T	H	HTH	— —
		T	HTT	———
TH	H	H	HHH	—⊖—
		T	HHT	— —
	T	H	HTH	— —
		T	HTT	———
TT	H	H	THH	— —
		T	THT	———
	T	H	TTH	———
		T	TTT	—✕—

As can easily be seen, there are three moving yangs, five yangs, one moving yin and seven yins – exactly as in the Yarrow Stick Method. Since this is easy, and mirrors the yarrow stick results, it seems wise to use this four coin method rather than the slightly

141

simpler three coins. It also seems more in keeping with the whole philosophy that we should turn a trinity into a quaternity. However, three coins are the usual method in all the literature, so if you prefer their simplicity it probably only makes a marginal difference.

Beads in a bag.

On the other hand I have also tried a 'beads in a bag' method without finding the results helpful, though at first sight one might expect them to be. In this system, 16 identically shaped beads are held in a bag from which one can be drawn at random without seeing it, and then replaced and the bag shaken. Five beads are, say, red and stand for simple yang: three are, say, orange and stand for moving yang. Seven are, say, green, representing simple yin, and the last is, say, blue representing moving yin. This theoretically gives the same probabilities as the yarrow sticks, but has never seemed satisfactory to me.

I can only assume that it is all too quick and random. Our unconscious mind is unable to exert any influence. In spinning coins we have an action that impacts on the result in subtle ways, and it is not impossible to feel that our mind may be influencing the result. Likewise, with the piles of yarrow sticks, the result depends on how we split the heaps, and again perhaps our unconscious mind can have an influence. But with picking an unseen bead there is no active input from us at all, so we really would be entirely in the realm of synchronicity.

Chapter ten

Jung's exposition of the concept of synchronicity.

The whole concept of an oracular device is anathema to a Western audience brought up on Newtonian mechanics, cause and effect, action and reaction and so on. How can it possibly be that spinning coins or separating yarrow sticks can lead to precisely the correct reading which is appropriate to the state of your unconscious at that moment? How can our unknown knowns become any the more known as a result of such an arcane experiment? And of course, on any 'normal-sized' experiment – with things we can see, things that have mass, matter, a demonstrable physicality – we are right to insist on causality, and therefore to dismiss any notion that tossed coins can fall in anything but a random, chance fashion.

Jung struggled with the concept of external, physical events apparently triggering, or being triggered by, an unconscious, psychic event happening at the same time, for many years – quite independently of any involvement in the I Ching. In his booklet '*Synchronicity – An Acausal Connecting Principle*' (translated by R F C Hull and first published in English in 1955) he gives several examples from his work with his clients of such happenings. One or two might help shed light on what he was trying to explain.

The first concerned a young woman patient who struggled to touch any of her unconscious archetypes (her unknown knowns), because of her intensely rational, scientific way of viewing the world. (Her animus, in Jung's archetypal terms). She was in the middle of relating a dream she had had which featured a 'golden scarab'. These are beetles which were worshipped by the ancient Egyptians, who made many golden amulets featuring the scarab. As she told of her dream, Jung became aware of a tapping noise behind him and turned to find an insect knocking against the window, although it was daylight outside and darker in the room. Opening the window he caught the beetle as it flew in, to find it was the common rose-chafer, the Swiss form of a scarab beetle. The coincidence was enough to break down the woman's emotional block and to allow her at last to be able to access her unconscious.

A second example he gives concerned the wife of one of his patients, a man in his fifties. She recalled that the deaths of both her mother and her grandmother had been accompanied by flocks of birds gathering outside the window of their death-chamber. Near the end of Jung's psychological treatment of her husband, he noticed the man seemed to have developed mild symptoms of heart disease. Jung sent him to a specialist who found no cause for alarm, and sent the man home. On the way he collapsed in the street, and as he was brought home dying his wife was already in a great state of anxiety because, soon after her husband had left to go to the specialist a flock of birds alighted on their roof.

And here's one from my own life. My wife and I were on holiday in Corfu, and visiting the small church on a cliff-top in Paleokastritsa. Out of the blue she was stricken by an overwhelming sadness and had to leave, quite distraught, sure that something was wrong with our daughter. Ringing her mobile brought no reply save the answerphone message, and it was many hours later that we learnt Sally was suffering a miscarriage at that very moment.

I don't expect you to be convinced by these hearsay events, but they are good examples of synchronicity as defined by Jung, where a physical event is matched by a concurrent psychic event. No causality is implied or possible, but the two events are meaningfully connected.

Jung comments: "To be entirely clear, synchronicity consists of two factors:

- An unconscious image comes into consciousness either directly (i.e. literally) or indirectly (symbolised or suggested) in the form of a dream, idea or premonition.

- An objective situation coincides with this content."
    (Synchronicity, p 44)

Jung goes on to say synchronicity can take three forms:
1) The coincidence of a certain psychic content with a corresponding objective process which is perceived to take place simultaneously.
2) The coincidence of a subjective psychic state with a phantasm (dream or vision) which later turns out to be a more or less faithful reflection of a 'synchronistic', objective event that took place more or less simultaneously, but at a distance.
3) The same, except that the event perceived takes place in the future and is represented in the present only by a phantasm that corresponds to it. *(ibid p 145)*

This is exactly the situation with the I Ching. The objective situation is the hexagram formed as a result of tossing coins or separating yarrow sticks, and the unconscious image is provided by the reading pointed to by the coins. Giving the process a name – synchronicity – does not, of course, make it any more understandable or rationally defensible, but it does put it into a context we may all recognise from our own experience. Time after time my wife and I find we are having the same thought at the same time, and whilst sometimes the thought may be a joint response to an external event I often find that I have come to the thought by a long process that I can recall, which may have 'triggered' in a synchronous way, the event that has stimulated the thought for my wife. And of course, sometimes the process has been initiated by her. I assume all of us have had similar experiences.

THE FRIENDSHIP BETWEEN JUNG AND PAULI.

We have already seen how Jung and Pauli used their long-standing friendship to mutual advantage, Pauli using Jung's psychological insights to feel his way to a deeper understanding of the fourth quantum number, an understanding beyond the narrow boundaries of science using instead Jung's 'archetypes'. And for his part, Jung was able to tap into Pauli's scientific and highly original mind to anchor his theories on the psyche on a firmer footing.

And, crucially, to fine-tune his theory of synchronicity – the word he coined to describe the acausal 'coincidence in space and time as meaning something more than mere chance, namely, a peculiar interdependence of objective events among themselves as well as with the subjective (psychic) state of the observer or observers.' *(Jung's foreword to Cary F Baynes' English version of Richard Wilhelm's translation of the I Ching, p xxiv).*

Synchronicity is a very 'quantum' philosophy, and yet, oddly, considering the friendship between the two men, the word quantum gets no mention in Jung's book on the subject. The nearest we get is a diagram agreed by the two, as shown below. However, this diagram, placed rather baldly in Jung's book, depends on a fundamental quantum concept: that of complementarity. This was first put forward by Niels Bohr, and states that many apparent opposites – particle vs. wave, position vs. momentum – are in fact complementary. That is to say they both need to be taken into account in order fully to comprehend the nature of the object being studied. Bohr went on to extend this principle philosophically in one of his lectures. "Complementarity bears a deep-going analogy to the general difficulty in the formation of human ideas, inherent in the distinction between subject and object." *(Makoto Katsumori: Niels Bohr's Complementarity. P 21)* In the Chinese yin and yang, complementary pairs of concepts define reality, and form the backbone of the I Ching.

Overleaf is the diagram finally (after several prototypes) agreed by the two men as showing complementarity in physics and in psychology.

Thus, on the vertical axis, the complementary principles that energy is indestructible at a quantum level versus the Newtonian Space-time continuum are shown, and a thorough understanding of our universe requires us to hold both in mind at all times.

```
                    Indestructible Energy
                            |
                            |
                            |
Constant Connection         |              Inconstant Connection
  through Effect             |              through Contingency,
   (Causality)  ————————————+————————      Equivalence, or 'Meaning'
                            |                  (Synchronicity)
                            |
                            |
                            |
                    Space-Time Continuum
```

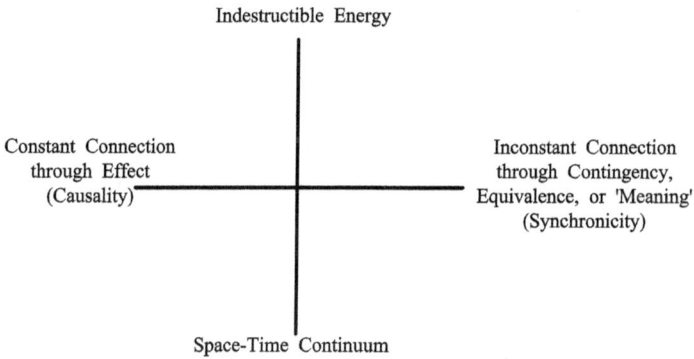

On the horizontal axis the complementarity is between our usual Newtonian notion of causality and the experience, nevertheless, of synchronicity. Again, a thorough understanding of reality requires us to hold both in mind.

Considering how very relevant Quantum Theory is to the almost inconceivable concept of a conscious (or unconscious) thought being intimately connected with an observable result, and considering that Wolfgang Pauli was one of the leading quantum physicists of his day, how might it be that Jung makes virtually no mention of it in his entire book on synchronicity? There seem to be several factors at play.

Firstly, Jung first developed his theory before he met Pauli, and was perhaps reasonably satisfied with his rationale without any complicated quantum influence. Also, quantum mechanics insists that its effects are entirely predictable (though paradoxical) and happen every time an experiment is made. Jung was describing an effect he conceived of as unpredictable and fortuitous. He was not primarily concerned with the I Ching, but with the archetypes of the unconscious in all their other forms of expression.

Secondly, Quantum theory was far from acceptable as anything more than a mathematical sleight-of-hand that produced accurate results in the infinitesimally small world of photons and electrons, but was best ignored on any larger scale. Einstein spent the last fifty years of his life trying to prove that quantum physics couldn't be acceptable as a model for anything bigger than photons.

The battle between him and Niels Bohr was at its peak in the 30s and 40s when Jung and Pauli were corresponding.

And thirdly, physicists in particular were unwilling to get embroiled in the philosophical aspects of quantum theory – the mantra was 'shut up and calculate' – and Pauli in particular was afraid that his scientific credentials might be blighted if Jung misused quantum physics in association with his name. Indeed, Pauli spent the latter part of his life hiding his preoccupation with psychology and the collective archetypes from his colleagues. Nevertheless, he and Jung together came closer than anyone else to a fusion of physics and psychology; between consciousness and quantum mechanics.

As an interesting post script Niels Bohr, who championed the quantum paradox against Einstein's sustained scepticism over a half-century, was awarded the Danish 'Order of the Elephant'. He incorporated the Taijitu, the yin yang symbol, on his coat of arms, along with the motto in Latin 'Contraria sunt complementa'. That is, roughly, **opposites are complementary!** Around the outside are linked elephants and castles, the collar of the order – the highest honour in Denmark.

Chapter eleven

How might quantum physics apply to synchronicity?

As was the case with DNA, we need an amateur appreciation of the effects Quantum Physics insist are a reality – though entirely paradoxical to our classical way of thinking. We will keep well away from the Maths, and concentrate only on one or two concepts. The first is trailered in Bohr's coat of arms, which figures both the Tai chi symbol and the motto 'Opposites are complementary'.

The first hints of the quantum paradox came with the question 'What is light?' The simple answer seemed to be that light was made up of particles: how else could it travel from the sun in the vacuum of space? These particles were called photons. However, even back in ancient Greece Aristotle proposed that light could be a wave, and suggested the space between the earth and the sun was filled with 'ether' which could oscillate in waves. Both theories had their supporters in the intervening centuries, till it became clear towards the end of the 19th Century that in fact both theories had to be held in tandem. As Einstein put it "It seems as though we must use sometimes the one theory and sometimes the other, while at times we may use either. We are faced with a new kind of difficulty. We have two contradictory pictures of reality; separately neither of them fully explains the phenomena of light, but together they do".

What could be more I Ching Taoist than that? We have

observed that the Tai Chi symbol, shows the seed of yang in the body of yin, and vice versa, and throughout the readings of the I Ching the theme of complementarity recurs time and again. Nothing is precisely one thing and not its opposite: every situation is a blend of those complementary opposites.

To demonstrate how photons could behave either as a particle or as a wave, early 20th Century scientists set up experiments and found that if they set out to prove light is a wave, it would indeed behave as a wave – and if they set out to prove it is a particle it would obligingly behave that way. In other words, the expectations of the observer dictated the result.

Quantum entanglement

The next big paradox that quantum physics threw up was too much even for Einstein, who christened it 'spooky action at a distance' and refused to accept it's reality for the rest of his long life. Briefly, quantum entanglement states that if two particles are created at the same time and place they are 'twins', and are 'entangled' inasmuch as each contributes to the pair's total measurement in all measureable areas – spin, polarisation, momentum and position. If the total spin is zero and one particle is measured and found to have a clockwise spin on a particular axis then the other will have an anti-clockwise spin on that axis.

Here's the rub… If an observer measures the spin of one of the twinned particles, he fixes it; just as measuring to prove a photon is a particle makes it behave as a particle, and vice versa for a wave. Before the measurement the photon had the potential to act either as a particle or as a wave; measuring collapses that potential. But if twins are entangled, collapsing the potential of one actually collapses the potential of the other, because they are twins. If the other were measured virtually at the same time, its state would be fixed, not with the potential it previously had to be either wave or particle. That is to say, the twin 'knows' instantaneously what its twin has decided to be – particle or wave, clockwise or anticlockwise spin. But by now, the twins could be millions of miles apart, theoretically, so how could that information be transmitted faster than the speed of light?

This argument, tuned to a much finer degree, kept Einstein and Niels Bohr on opposing sides for the rest of their lives, but has now been comprehensively settled both mathematically and experimentally to confirm that entanglement is a quantum reality.

Now, when we get to looking at our own brains, we enter the same sub-atomic field as is inhabited by photons – we are in the quantum world. And we are in a world where multiple 'twins' are being constantly created, as the brain is formed before birth by almost infinite cell division. Our neuron structures at sub-molecular level must, by definition, be quantum entangled, because they are constantly being produced by a cell splitting in two, just as physicists split particles to study entanglement. Now we might just come full-circle, back to Jung's collective unconscious.

You will remember that in chapter eight I hypothesised that, if the collective unconscious is a reality it must be transmitted in our DNA, and that, to be unvaried by parentage, it must be in the mitochondrial DNA which is passed mother to daughter without variation (and of course to son, but they don't pass it on). This could (and I accept the very tentative nature of this argument) lead to quantum entanglement between all people.

This could also lead to the sort of synchronicity sometimes observed between people – my wife and daughter for instance in the example on page 144. This is entanglement in the unconscious of both which, if brought to consciousness leads to a 'knowing' that something is amiss. In the case of mother and daughter, of course, there is also entanglement in the conscious brain, since they also share non-mitochondrial DNA and hence entangled neuron structures.

In quantum terms entanglement between twinned particles is inevitable: in human terms synchronicity is rare and spasmodic. This is only to be expected, given the hypothesis that most cross-human entanglement is within the unconscious. For a synchronistic event to happen, between people, the event would need to be important enough for the conscious mind of the sufferer to 'inform' her unconscious, for the entanglement to 'inform' the unconscious of the rest of the world's human population, and for the unconscious of the one person who might care to find a way of informing her conscious mind. Not surprising, then, that such events are rare – but by no means non-existent.

Might it also be that quantum entanglement is at the root of the collective forces observable when a crowd gathers? In much the same way as a swarm of bees is clearly entangled, or the magnificently wheeling flight of a huge flock of starlings, or a stampede of cattle, so a crowd of people takes on a corporate identity which subsumes the individual identities. If the neuron structures at sub-molecular level in everyone's unconscious are entangled because they are inherited from a single 'Mitochondrial Eve' then we might well expect the observable crowd mentality displayed at football grounds, pop concerts and on the battlefield.

In his book *Entangled Minds: extrasensory experiences in a quantum reality* Dean Radin, Senior Scientist at the Institute of Noetic Sciences, in Petaluma, California, USA, explores the thesis that world-wide response to huge global events such as the funeral of Pope John Paul II or 9/11 actually affects measurable events such as the output from the various Random Number Generators across the world. (*Chapter 11*).

This thesis may be at the root of the two Jungian examples on page 143. There the synchronicity is between the natural world and the patient/client. Is there any way that quantum entanglement could be involved? In the case of the woman convinced by the presence of the flock of birds that her husband was dying the birds may conceivably have been 'summoned' by her husband. Her husband's distress could be transmitted to her as above, with the birds as an aid to helping her unconscious contact her conscious mind. The scarab, and any other form of pre-cognition, which Jung catalogues as being a part of synchronicity, seems of a different order and is covered by Radin in his chapter on Presentiment (*ibid. chapter 10*).

Entanglement and the I Ching
Jung felt, but could never really show, that synchronicity might play a part in the oracular aspect of the I Ching. Can we show any possible

mechanism where quantum entanglement might somehow enable our unconscious brain to create an appropriate I Ching reading for the situation we may find ourselves in? Somewhat to my discomfort I find it easier to suggest for the yarrow stick method than for tossing coins, but in practice have found coin-tossing consistently helpful.

In chapter nine I observed that the 'beans in a bag' method of obtaining a hexagram and hence a reading never seemed to produce sensible results, even though in probability terms it was identical to the yarrow sticks. I speculated that because everything was quick and out of sight the unconscious had no opportunity to affect the result. This I think may be the key. I can believe that in separating 48 yarrow sticks into two piles the unconscious might be able to direct the conscious mind and the physical action of separation so as to produce piles with the 'right' numbers in for the effect that the unconscious 'knows' is appropriate to the question the conscious mind is asking. I am much more doubtful that it would be able to direct the tossing of coins – a much more random action. Not only so, but with the yarrow sticks if the unconscious 'knows' the result it wants, it has two opportunities after the first separation to modify the line eventually chosen – and with diminishing piles of sticks and hence an easier opportunity to separate them appropriately. Here entanglement might well be the mechanism that connects the unconscious and the conscious, so allowing the unconscious to direct the conscious.

Also, as I showed on page 124, and expand in the next chapter, the readings, like the codons in DNA, are in groups. So just as a ribosome can read sometimes as many as six different codons to produce the same amino acid, so our unconscious could point us to several different readings which would give us food for thought.

Now I have to recognise that I have strayed far from the basic concept of synchronicity – that it is non-causal – and have started to dream up possible causal paths! But these are not causal in the classical sense, but in the quantum sense that entanglement 'causes' the twin particle – or in our case neuron structures at the sub-molecular level – to behave as if caused by the experiment on its twin. What I am suggesting is that the I Ching provides a mechanism for our unconscious to interact with our conscious mind, and that it does so in a way which mirrors the way ribosomes produce amino acids by 'reading' codons. Somehow, perhaps by entanglement with the conscious neurons, it produces either the precise I Ching reading or at least one of the group which is related.

Twenty years ago this would all be in the realms of science fiction, but our understanding of genes, the brain, and of DNA itself is becoming much more complex. There have been several scientific papers published which study quantum entanglement in biological molecules and it is generally considered proved at experimental level. (Gilmore and McKenzie 2005; Plenio and Huelga 2008; Thorwart et al. 2009). Genes, long thought to be unchangeable in a life, are now known to be changeable by some life experiences. For a lay study of this new science of Epigenics, see *Identically Different – why you can change your genes*, by Tim Spector. ISBN: 978-1-7802-2090-1. For a paper specifically on our subject, see Igor V. Limar's *C.G. Jung's synchronicity and quantum entanglement*, published in the journal 'NeuroQuantology' – (2011) Volume 9, Issue 2, pp 313-321. I may be flying kites, but there is a fair wind!

Chapter Twelve

The grouping of hexagrams

We have seen, in chapter seven, that in the 8x8 matrix based on the binary numbers, the amino acids group in exactly the same way as they do in the standard bio-chemical tables. If it transpires that the hexagram readings also group into recognisable themes in the same way, it would consolidate the assertion that there is a fundamental similarity between the patterns. We start with a reminder of the 'great chart'.

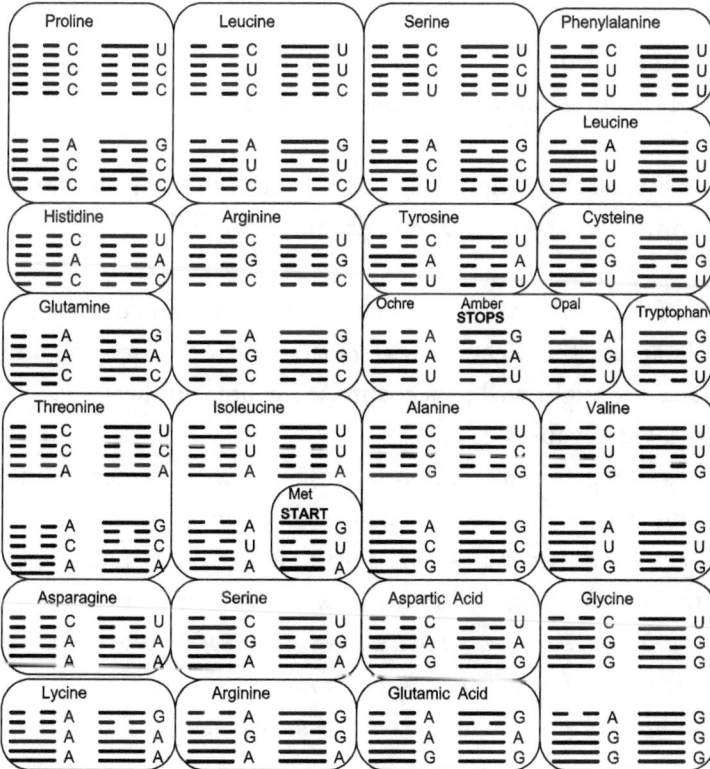

Proline	Leucine	Serine	Phenylalanine
C C C — U C C	C U C — U U C	C C U — U C U	C U U — U U U
			Leucine
A C C — G C C	A U C — G U C	A C U — G C U	A U U — G U U
Histidine	**Arginine**	**Tyrosine**	**Cysteine**
C A C — U A C	C C G — U C G	C A U — U A U	C G C — U G C
Glutamine		Ochre / Amber **STOPS**	Opal / **Tryptophan**
A A G — G A C	A G C — G G C	A A G — G A U	A G G — G G U
Threonine	**Isoleucine**	**Alanine**	**Valine**
C C A — U C A	C U A — U U A	C C G — U C G	C U G — U U G
	Met START		
A C A — G C A	A U A — G U A	A C G — G C G	A U G — G U G
Asparagine	**Serine**	**Aspartic Acid**	**Glycine**
C A A — U A A	C G A — U G A	C A G — U A G	C G G — U G G
Lycine	**Arginine**	**Glutamic Acid**	
A A A — G A A	A G A — G G A	A A G — G A G	A G G — G G G

Looking first at the group corresponding to Proline, in the top left corner, there are two things to note immediately.

1) The codons are all the four beginning CC_. (The codons are written from the bottom up, remember.) That is, the last base in the codon doesn't affect which amino acid is produced, in this case. CCA, CCU, CCC and CCG all produce Proline.

2) In hexagram terms, the four hexagrams are all the possible combinations of Earth ☷ ☷ and Mountain ☶ ☶.

This pattern is discernible in the groups of four down the principal diagonal.

For Arginine, all the codons begin CG_, and the four hexagrams are all the combinations of Water ☵ and Wood/wind ☴.

For Alanine, all the codons begin GC_, and the hexagrams are the combinations of Thunder ☳ and Fire ☲.

For Glycine, all the codons begin GG_ , and the four hexagrams are all the combinations of Heaven ☰ and Lake ☱.

That takes us down the principal diagonal. Since the readings generally access the archetypes associated with the two trigrams in a hexagram, we might well expect similar readings in these cases, and in fact this is observable.

Looking first at the 'proline' hexagrams, all combinations of Earth and Mountain, we can expect the four readings to use the metaphors and attributes of Earth and Mountain, which are respectively *The Receptive is the earth, the mother. It is cloth, a kettle, frugality; it is level, a cow with a calf, a large wagon, form, the multitude, a shaft. Among the various kinds of soil it is the black.*

Main attribute: yielding. Associated animal: cow.'

'Keeping still is the mountain; it is a bypath; it means little stones, doors and openings, fruits and seeds, eunuchs and watchmen, the fingers. It is the dog, the rat and the various types of black-billed birds. Among trees it signifies the firm and gnarled (e.g. hawthorn).

Main attribute: standstill. Associated animal: dog.'

We should be able to expect readings advocating resilience in the face of hardship, a feminine acceptance of one's lot – an eschewal of aggressive yang reactions; and this is indeed what we get.

Proline: Nos. 2, 23, 15 & 52

2: The Receptive.

Yielding and devoted. Image of the mare. Consistent seriousness.

23. Splitting apart (Disintegration).

This is a condition of the times – bad things happen. The right behaviour in such times is inner docility and devotion, and outward stillness. Although usually unpleasant, times of disintegration are a necessary part of things and should be seen as precursors to better times.

15. Modesty.

Moderation in all things. Men hate arrogance, and love modesty.

52. Keeping still.

Again, reacting appropriately to the demands of the time. There is a time to keep still, quiet, calm, and if this is one of them, take notice! We need to be very aware of our inner state in order to achieve this stillness, but it is worth the effort.

Common theme: Acceptance of one's lot – not 'kicking against the pricks'. All four readings stress the yin aspects of life; acceptance, a lack of showy aggression, going with the flow, not standing out.

The second set of four, corresponding to Arginine, combine Water ☵ and Wood/wind ☴. Their metaphors and attributes are respectively

The abysmal is water, ditches, ambush, bending and straightening out, bow and wheel. Among men it means the melancholy, those with sick hearts, those

with earache. It is the blood sign; it is red. Among horses it means those with beautiful backs, those with wild courage, those which let their hair hang, those with thin hoofs, those which stumble. Among chariots it means those with many defects. It is penetration, the moon. It means thieves. Among varieties of wood it means those which are firm and have much pith.

Main attribute: dangerous. Associated animal: pig.

The gentle is wood, wind, the eldest daughter, the guideline, work. It is the white, the long, the high; it is advance and retreat, the undecided, scent or odour. Among men it means the grey-haired, those with broad foreheads; it means those with much white in their eyes; it means those who gain, so that in the market they get threefold value. Finally, it is the sign of vehemence.

Main attribute: penetration. Associated animal: the cock.

We should expect readings to be more pro-active than those for proline, with more of a yang feel to them.

Arginine: Nos. 29, 59, 48, & 57.

29. The abysmal.

An objective situation brought about by the times. When we are confronted by external difficulties we should take our cue from how water behaves when obstructed. It fills in cavities and holes then moves on to the next obstruction. It plunges over precipices when necessary, always retaining its essential nature. So, do what must be done with thoroughness. Go forward. Do not tarry in danger.

59. Dispersion (The Dissolving).

Religion, at its best, disperses a man's egotism, dissolves the barriers between us and unites us. We need religious rites, splendour and sacred music to help in this removal of the ego and union of like minds.

48. The Well.

The well is the unchanging fundamentals that exist independently of external change. Basic human nature is unchanging, and the root of the divine within humanity. To draw on this source, however, requires deep penetration: one must be neither shallow nor careless in self-development.

57. The Gentle (The Penetrating).

Gentleness succeeds through having a clearly defined goal. It achieves its purpose by ceaseless influence, acting always in the same direction: adaptable yet consistent.

Gentleness shows depth of character. Through gentleness one can weigh things and come to understand their inner nature without being in the forefront oneself. It can take special circumstances into account, and make exceptions, without being inconsistent.

Common theme: Being thorough in order to achieve a goal. Superficiality will achieve nothing, either in a difficult situation, in religion, in seeking out our deepest thoughts and feelings, or in tackling our deepest problems. This theme of making the best of a difficult situation is repeated in the other block of two.

Whilst this block of four on the principal diagonal just combine Water and Wood in all four possible ways, there is another group of two on the bottom line of the table, , and . Here, Water is first paired with Heaven, then Wood is paired with Heaven, maintaining the Water and Wood archetypes observed in the first group of four. These two give readings:

5. Waiting.

Again, patience, moderation. Don't be in too much of a hurry, the time will come.

9. The taming power of the gentle.

Situations where we can only exert minimal influence. Use what is possible, friendly persuasion, gentleness.

Joint Common theme: Being in difficult situations, and having to call on all our deepest reserves in order to move forward and attain a goal.

The third set of four, corresponding to Alanine, combines all permutations of Fire ☲ and Thunder ☳. We must surely expect a much more yang feel to these, as their attributes are, for Fire:

The Clinging is fire, the sun, lightning, the middle daughter. It means coats of mail and helmets, lances and weapons. Among men it means the big-bellied. It is the sign of dryness. It means the tortoise, the crab, the snail, the mussel, the hawkbill tortoise. Among trees it means those which dry out in the upper part of the trunk.

Main attribute: dependence. Associated animal: pheasant.

And for Thunder:

The arousing is thunder, the dragon. It is dark yellow, a spreading out, a great road, the eldest son. It is decisive and vehement; it is bamboo that is green and young, it is reed and rush. Among horses it signifies those which can neigh well, those with white hind legs, those which gallop, those with a star on the forehead. And among useful plants it is the pod-bearing ones. Finally, it is the strong, that which grows luxuriantly.

Main attribute: movement. Associated animal: dragon.

Alanine: Nos. 51, 21, 55 & 30.

51. The Arousing (Shock).

A strange one, based on the fear of God in some way. Some shock revelation inspires fear in our hearts: it is how we deal with this fear that is important.

21. Biting through (Judging).

Judgement is necessary in a society, and must combine both hardness and excitement with clarity and gentleness. Another common factor in the I Ching is that of 'Proportionality'. Judgement and penalty must always be proportionate: enough to deter, not too much so as to crush completely and arouse resentment in many.

55. Abundance (Fullness).

Again, a product of the times, and again, beware because inevitably good times will be followed by harder times. All things wax and wane in the course of time. Abundance cannot be maintained permanently, and it can only endure at all if ever more people are brought to share in it; otherwise it will turn into its opposite, emptiness.

30. The clinging.

Unless we have something to cling to – the forces of spiritual life – we burn out. Human life is conditioned and limited. Before one can achieve success one must accept these limitations and make oneself dependent on the harmonious and beneficent forces of the cosmos. Only by cultivating an attitude of compliance and voluntary dependence can one acquire clarity without sharpness or arrogance and find one's place in the world.

Common theme: These four readings, combining Thunder and Fire in all the four ways possible, seem to refer to how society is to be regulated if its people are to have good lives. Thus religion and the law are seen as critical, and the need for society to be fair to all its members.

The last of this type are the hexagrams corresponding to Glycine, all the possible pairings of Lake ☱ and Heaven ☰. Again, there is a lot of Yang involved, and their attributes are, for Lake: *The joyous is the lake, the youngest daughter. It is a sorceress; it is a mouth and tongue. It means smashing and breaking apart; dropping off and bursting open. Among the kinds of soil it is the hard and salty. Among animals it is the sheep or goat.*

> *Main attribute: pleasure. Associated animal: sheep.*

And for Heaven: *The Creative is heaven. It is round, it is the prince, the father, jade, metal, cold, ice; it is deep red, a good horse, an old horse, a wild horse, tree fruit.* Later commentaries add to the list: *it is straight, it is the dragon, the upper garment, the word.*

> *Main attribute: strength. Associated animal: horse.*

Glycine: Nos. 58, 10, 43 & 1.

58. The Joyous.

Joy is good and infectious, and can achieve great things among men, but it must not be allowed to degenerate into uncontrolled mirth.

The best way of government is to lead the people joyously. Men's hearts won by friendship and joy are true followers.

10. Conduct (Comportment).

The way to deal with intractable people – pleasantly, with good humour and manners. Don't fight fire with fire!

43. Break-through (Resoluteness).

Concerned with the fight between good and evil. (Or, interestingly, between passion and reason, which it claims cannot co-exist.) In the struggle against evil there are four rules which we cannot disregard, and as usual these are based on moderation.

- Outright defiance is counselled against. Resolution must be based on a union of strength and goodwill.
- Compromise with evil is not possible. It must be honestly discredited, not least in one's own passions and shortcomings.
- Direct force must not be used for it leads to entanglement in hatred and passion, and hence we lose in the end. As long as we fight evil, blow for blow, it will prevail.
- Finally, the best way to fight evil is to make energetic progress in the good.

1. The Creative.

Each end is a new beginning. Strong on perseverance, on completing things in their due time. Time is the instrument of the creative force – the appropriate time for action, and the slow working out of that action over time.

Common theme: These four readings are strongly Yang types, being all the combinations of Lake and Heaven, and yet counsel against the over-emphasis of yang. Thus joy must not degenerate into the buffoonery of a barrack-room; intractable opponents must be dealt with gently, and with humour, and every creative act needs perseverance to bring it to fruition. (1% inspiration, 99% perspiration).

Chapter thirteen

Other groups of four hexagrams.

There are four other groups of four hexagrams corresponding to groups of four codons all producing the same amino acid – those for Leucine, Serine, Threonine, and Valine, and in all cases once again we note that the first two letters of their codons are identical. That is, in Leucine for instance, all four codons begin CU_, in Serine UC_ and so on. However, the hexagram patterns are more complex, though interestingly the same particular complexity in all five examples. Looking at Leucine, the group is

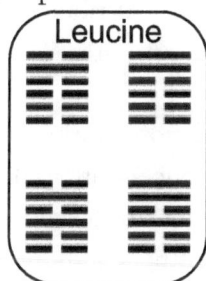

The pattern is Water over Earth and Thunder; and Wood over Earth and Thunder, or in general notation:

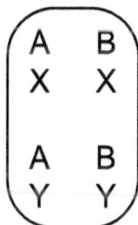

$$\begin{array}{cc} A & B \\ X & X \\ A & B \\ Y & Y \end{array}$$

For Leucine A= Water ☵, B= Wood ☴, X= Earth ☷, Y= Mountain ☶.

For Serine A= Thunder ☳, B= Fire ☲, X= Earth ☷, Y = Mountain ☶ .

163

For Threonine A= Earth ☷, B= Mountain ☶, X=Thunder ☳,
Y=Fire ☲

For Valine A= Lake ☱, B= Heaven ☰, X=Thunder ☳,
Y=Fire ☲

We might well not expect all four readings to have a common theme,

   A   **B**

for **X** contains completely different trigrams from **Y**. And yet, looking at all the various hexagrams a common theme can be seen for each group of four. We start with Leucine, with its four

hexagrams ䷇, ䷓, ䷦ and ䷴. These give the readings below:

Leucine: Nos. 8, 20, 39 & 53

8. Holding together.

Leaders and their necessary attributes: sublimity, constancy and perseverance. A wise leader cultivates relationships.

20. Contemplation (View).

There is an element of religion, spirituality, in this one. It is by the power of deepest inner concentration that religious contemplation develops in great men. From this a hidden spiritual power emanates from them that influences others without their being aware of how it happens.

39. Obstruction.

When we are confronted by obstacles that cannot be overcome directly we should not press on regardless into danger, nor idly just keep still, but should yield and retreat, carefully, only in preparation for overcoming the obstruction. If this retreat seems to lead away from the ultimate goal we need the will to persevere, to hold to our inner purpose.

53. Development. (Gradual progress).

Gradual development is the correct way to progress in many aspects of life. Relationships need time to develop, as do negotiations with others. Above all, self-development, the correct and careful cultivation of our own personality is critical, and takes time. But the very gradualness of development makes perseverance essential. It alone prevents slow progress dwindling to nothing.

Common theme: Relationships, and the correct way to form and conduct them. Also the need to persevere in and with relationships. There is also an element of gradual influence permeating each reading.

Before we move on we should note that the amino acid Leucine is also produced by another set of two codons – UUA and UUG. It would be very telling with regard to the fundamental relationship between DNA and the I Ching if the two corresponding hexagrams also have a theme in common with the four above. ䷟ and ䷞ give the readings below:

Leucine: Nos. 31, 33

31. Influence (wooing).

Moderation again – this time in wooing, either between the sexes or in politics or life generally. 'By keeping still within, whilst experiencing joy without, one can prevent joy from going to excess and hold it within proper bounds.' Steadfastness, and the stronger deferring to the weaker – again a recurrent theme.

33. Retreat (Withdrawal).

Success lies in being able to retreat at the right time and in the right way. Again it is to do with the times: there is a right time to retreat, and we need to be able to distinguish between it and the time to stand and fight. Retreat, when necessary, is not weakness but a sign of maturity.

Common theme: These are indeed of a piece with the previous four: indeed, 33 Retreat and 39 Obstruction are very similar. It is beginning to look as if there is a very real correlation between the codon groups and the corresponding groups of hexagrams.

Moving on to the hexagrams corresponding to the codons which produce Serine, we notice there are again two groups, the four on the top rows of the table and two near the bottom. In this case there is very little apparent connection, for the top group are made from the trigrams for Thunder, Fire, Earth and Mountain, while the lower pair combine Water, Wood and Lake in various ways. Only Heaven is not represented here. And yet, comparing the readings does show a common theme running through all six, as shown below:

Serine: Nos. 16, 62, 35 & 56 in one block. 60 & 61 in the other

16. Enthusiasm.

To arouse enthusiasm, one must adjust oneself to the character of those one wishes to lead. Only such laws as are rooted in popular sentiment can be enforced: otherwise they arouse resentment.

62. Great smallness.

Exceptional modesty and conscientiousness are sure to succeed; but it is important to ensure they do not become empty form, fawning and servile. They must always be combined with appropriate dignity in personal behaviour, if one is not to throw oneself away.

Again, one must understand the demands of the time in order to offset its difficulties. But one should recognise that one cannot count on success, for the requisite strength is missing. Don't strive after lofty things, but hold to the lowly.

35. Easy progress.

If we can combine clarity of thought with devotion to the task in hand we make good, and easy, progress. Conversely, if progress is frustrated and difficult, it may well be that we are lacking clarity of purpose or the necessary devotion to our task.

56. The Wanderer (The Seeker).

The picture is of moving on, things that should be of short duration. Things such as penalties, imprisonment, lawsuits, arguments, conflict: none of these should be allowed to be protracted. If a man is a wanderer he needs to be cautious and reserved, for he is always on others' territory. Only by being obliging will he win success.

Common theme: Ways of getting things done, of persuading others to join in a venture. And an element of being the outsider, the one making things happen. Also elements of the Law, and how it should be applied, which chime with the separate block, below.

60. Limitation (Due measure).
Applied to money and economy. Limitations are tiresome, but valuable. It is good to live economically in normal times, for then we are prepared for times of want.
In setting limits for ourselves we must observe due measure (moderation again!). He who seeks to impose galling limitations on his own nature brings injury to himself, and if he tries it on others they will only rebel. So even limitation must be limited!
61. Inner Truth.
A humble heart, free of all prejudice, and therefore open to the truth. This is concerned with government and the law, and also in our day to day judgements of others. Unless we are to be superficial in these judgements we must let the other's mind and circumstances soak into us.

      Common theme: Keeping oneself pure, free from prejudice and the trappings of wealth. These two common themes share the strand of being a bit of an outsider, accommodating oneself to society's norms in order to help that society make progress.

The third of this type of group corresponds to Threonine,
䷗, ䷚, ䷟ and ䷏, giving the readings below:

Threonine: Nos. 24, 27, 36 & 22.
24. Return (The turning point).
Again, a condition of the times, and the natural end-point of disintegration. Things are beginning to get better. However, we need to be pro-active, to make decisions, and to act decisively.

27. Providing nourishment.

If we wish to know a man we have only to observe on whom he bestows his care and what sides of his nature he cultivates. Small men cultivate their lower natures: wise men cultivate their higher natures.

36. Darkening of the light.

There are times when circumstances are unfavourable: but we should not allow ourselves to be swept along with them, or lose our steadfastness. The answer is to maintain our inner light whilst remaining outwardly yielding and tractable. Sometimes it is necessary to hide this inner light, and persevere only in our inner consciousness.

22. Grace (Adornment).

Gracefulness is pleasing, but is not the essential or fundamental thing. It is only the external ornament, and so should be used sparingly. True gracefulness is a combination of inner clarity and outward quietness.

Common theme: It is not easy to detect a common theme here. 24 & 36 are obviously linked together, as waiting for the light at the end of the tunnel; and 27 and 22 are linked by the idea of knowing someone by how he treats himself – what does he eat, read, listen to; and how does he dress and so on. But there is an element of being prepared by how one treats oneself affecting one's ability to weather the storms of life.

The next group of four is slightly different in that while three of the codons produce Isoleucine, the other is actually Methionine, produced by the 'Start' codon, AUG. This critical codon is the trigger that begins the reading of a string of mRNA by the ribosomes. Is its hexagram completely different from the other three, or is there a subtle correspondence? The four hexagrams in question are

▤, ▤, ▤ and ▤ for Methionine. A brief overview detects the trigrams for Water and Wood as the upper trigrams, Thunder and Fire as the lower. The corresponding readings are:

Isoleucine: Nos. 3, 42, 63 and for Methionine (start) No. 37.

3. Difficulty at the beginning.

Beginnings are chaotic – which strand to follow, what to disregard? Perseverance and assistance from others are the prime recommended requirements here.

42. Increase.

Again, the theme is of great undertakings – beginnings – and of joint enterprise.

63. Order (After completion).

In a sense, the other end of the spectrum, when an undertaking is complete. The image (Water over Fire) is of a kettle on the boil. Tea is almost ready, but still care is needed not to mix the two constituents.

37. The family.

In one sense this draws together the other three readings, for a family certainly begins chaotically, as husband and wife start a life together. Later, normally, there is indeed increase, as children are born. Later still, there is a sense of order after completion, as the family is complete, the children grow, and father and mother have grown to know each other completely. Constant care is still the order of the day, though, as families can go adrift very easily, with profound repercussions for all members.

Common theme: 'The family' seems to me to be the common theme, and very apt as the Start hexagram.

The last group of four codons all producing one Amino Acid is that for Valine, where the codons all start GU_. The corresponding hexagrams are ▦, ▦, ▦ and ▦. These produce readings No. 17, 25, 49 and 13. Lake, Heaven, Thunder and Fire are the trigrams involved, so with an eye on their attributes shown in chapter five we might expect the common theme, if there is one, to be of a Yang nature, featuring the necessary breakages, injuries, tears, and collateral damage attendant on creativity.

17. Following.

The judgement warns that inciting a movement, producing a following, is fraught with danger. We must take great care that followers are not harmed or preyed upon by the leaders.

25. Innocence.

This one is to do with our ulterior motives. We each have a good guide – our conscience – within us which will guide out instinctive actions; but as soon as we become conscious of those actions there is the danger of selfishness and manipulation. The counsel is to remain true to our conscience at all times.

49. Revolution (Fundamental change).

This one is the extreme form of the two previous readings, covering events from social upheaval to outright war. Collateral damage, blood, sweat and tears are inevitable, and care of the first order is needed at all times to ensure motives and actions remain as pure as they can be.

13. Fellowship.

Again this is about leadership, and this time the stress is on a leader's need to be flexible, yielding when necessary, yet steadfast and enlightened.

Common theme: As we foresaw, from the attributes of the trigrams, these are all to do with the need to respect others, and in particular the weaker, when leading a group into action. The dangers are repeated in each of the readings, and are dangers all leaders should have at the forefront of their deliberations.

Chapter fourteen

The groups of two hexagrams.

From the great chart (page 155) we can see nine further groups of two hexagrams corresponding to pairs of codons (as well as the separated pairs for Serine, Arginine and Leucine already considered). In all cases the pair share the bottom trigram, which may well give rise to a common theme in each particular pairing. Taking them in order as we move along the binary numbers which are the basis of the table, we come first to Phenylalanine, with the codons UUA and

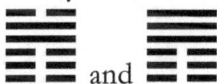

UUG, and the hexagrams ䷬ and ䷋ - Lake over Earth and Heaven over Earth respectively. These correspond to readings 45 and 12. Although there seems little difference in the hexagrams – just the sixth line – the readings give a very different feel to what is, in many ways, the same scenario: that of the natural gathering together of people, whether because they are family or class. The first is in a major key, joyful and productive: the second in a minor key, melancholy and depressive.

Phenylalanine: Nos. 45 and 12
45. Gathering together.
The people gathering together are energetic, intent on great things, of a natural common frame of mind. There is however a warning of the danger of either strife or stagnation in such a gathering.
12. Stagnation.
This is often the end-point of the movement described above. The energy has been dissipated, the great things perhaps completed, but a sense of emptiness pervades. 'Where there is no vision, the people perish' *(Proverbs 29:18)*.

Common theme: These are two sides of the same coin, and warn that everything needs continuous renewal in order not to stagnate and die. We see the truth of this in all gathering together of people with a shared interest: the club, society, nation even, goes through phases, ebbing and flowing, needing energy to revive its fortunes.

Next is Histidine, codons CAC and CAU, with corresponding hexagrams ䷆ and ䷃ – Earth over Water and Mountain over Water. Again there seems little difference – just the sixth line – but as with the case above at first sight the readings seem diametrically opposed. The first is No. 7, The Army, conjuring images of discipline and fixed ways of doing things. The second is No. 4, Immaturity (Youthful Folly) – almost the antithesis of the Army! And indeed, as with the case above, the very opposition is the connecting principle, the common theme.

Histidine: Nos. 7 and 4.
7. The Army.
The image is of great strength stored up in case of need, groundwater under the earth. But discipline is vital if this force is to be useful; the leaders must hold the force in control, not allowing unbridled or unlawful action.
4.Immaturity (Youthful folly).
The image is of a stream emerging at the foot of a mountain, not knowing which direction to set off in. Discipline is needed, a teacher must be sought out… and importantly, his answers need to be heeded. However, the teacher must wait till the youth is ready to seek knowledge, otherwise his guidance will be ignored.

Common theme: The need for discipline, for guidance.

Tyrosine is formed by the codons UAC and UAU, and the corresponding hexagrams are ䷧ and ䷔, respectively Thunder over Water and Fire over Water. Danger is surely in the air, with Water as the abysmal, and Thunder as a shock, and Fire including lightning in its attributes. The readings are Nos. 40 and 21.

Tyrosine: Nos. 40 and 21.

40. Deliverance.

Here the situation is moving out of danger. Just as thunder and rain relieve atmospheric tension, making buds burst open, so in our own lives release from burdensome pressures and stress has a liberating effect. The counsel is to return to normal life as soon as possible.

21. Biting through (Judgement).

In this case we are making an effort (biting through) to bring about the change, the move out of danger. Again, the advice is that normal service should be restored as soon as possible.

Common theme: Some times are dangerous, either from natural causes or from man's own destructive impulses. We need to face up to the danger, overcome it, and return to stable life as soon as we can.

Cysteine has, as its formative codons, UGC and UGU, and the corresponding hexagrams are ䷮ (Lake over Water) and ䷅ (Heaven over Water). Water's presence alerts us to the likelihood of adverse situations, and we are not wrong, for the two readings are indeed warnings to mitigate and escape as soon as practicable. Respectively, they are:

Cysteine: Nos. 47 and 6

47. Oppression.

The image, a lake with all the water having run out of the bottom, is of an exhaustion beyond normal tiredness. It is a time of adversity, and how we face that adversity is all important, for it will determine whether we emerge strengthened by the experience or allow ourselves to be overwhelmed by it.

6. Conflict.

Similarly, conflict is an adversity to be faced, and again, how we react and the steps we take to turn conflict into consensus is critical.

Common theme: There are times when everything seems to be against us. We need to recognise the times for what they are and react constructively to find our way through or round the obstacles.

Next on the list is Glutamine, with its codons CAA and CAG, associated hexagrams ䷭ (Earth over Wood/Wind) and ䷑ (Mountain over Wood/Wind). With the attributes in mind, from chapter five, we should expect gentler situations than for the previous pair, with Wood/Wind representing gentle penetration, Earth the Receptive mother figure, and Mountain stillness. Surely these will be favourable pairings. In order, they are:

Glutamine: Nos. 46 and 18.

46. Pushing upward.

This is certainly favourable, with the image of new growth penetrating, or pushing up, through the earth. Pushing upwards is made possible not by violence, but by modesty and adaptability, just as a plant feels its way round any obstacle to its progress.

18. Removing corruption (Decay).

The reading advocates care and caution in clearing out decay to allow for new growth. We need to take care to understand the nature of the corruption we wish to tackle, and then to act decisively but warily to remove it completely. Only then can the new ways be undertaken successfully.

Common theme: Making progress carefully but decisively. Nevertheless, not vaunting oneself at the expense of the old, but proceeding modestly.

Moving now to the bottom two rows of the great table, we have four more pairs to consider (Serine and Arginine having been amalgamated previously to their larger groups of four). Asparagine and Aspartic Acid both have the Lake trigram ☱ as their lower element, so we might expect some aspect of joyousness in both pairs. Asparagine also has the gentler trigrams ☷ ☷, Earth, and ☶ ☶, Mountain as the upper elements, so once again we might expect favourable situations for its two hexagrams ䷒ and ䷨. They are:

Asparagine: Nos. 19 and 41.
19. Approach (Becoming great).
The Judgement reads

> *A time of joyous progress brings favour*
> *One should persevere in the right*
> *For its end will surely come.*

Times are good, but we are warned to 'make hay while the sun shines', for as ever with the I Ching, we are warned that all things must pass, and change is inescapable.

41. Decrease.
At first sight, almost the opposite of the situation above, and indeed in one sense it is. Where in the previous reading the times were propitious, here the opposite is true: the times are against us, decrease is all around. Nevertheless, the advice is similar, for the Judgement reads:

> *At a time of decrease*
> *Sincerity brings great good fortune. No blame.*
> *For God accepts the simplest sacrifice.*

The advised action is the same: persevere. The warning is the same: all things will change.

Common theme: Whatever the external circumstances we should act to make the best of the situation, always aware that times must, and will, change.

The other pair on this line are for Aspartic Acid, with GAC and GAU as its codons. The corresponding hexagrams are

☷ , The Marrying Maiden (Love) and ☲ , Opposition. These do not look, on the face of it, likely bedfellows. Indeed, one might have expected The Marrying Maiden to partner Approach (above) and Opposition to partner Decrease (above). Have the pairings got mixed up? Let's look at the small print for this pair.

Aspartic Acid: Nos. 54 and 38.
54. The Marrying Maiden (Love).
The Judgement reads:

> *The marrying maiden: joyous in movement.*
> *Love is the basis of all true union:*
> *In heaven and earth, in the cycle of life,*
> *In the trusting reserve of a loving wife.*

And the Judgement for *38. Opposition.* reads:

> *Opposition in small matters leads to union*
> *And thence to good fortune.*
> *Great indeed is the effect*
> *Of the time of opposition.*

The expansion of the Judgement makes its similarity to the previous reading quite explicit, saying: 'The oppositions of heaven and earth, of spirit and nature, of man and woman, when reconciled, bring about the creation and reproduction of life.'

Common theme: the complementarity of opposites, and their necessity for the creation of life. Love and opposition are not mutually exclusive: on the contrary they are inevitable bedfellows. Love and opposition are needed to effect deep change within each of us. We need to be opposed, confronted, but only if it is done by someone who loves us is the desired change effective.

The last two sets of pairs, on the bottom line of the great table have Heaven ☰ as the lower trigram, so we must expect some yang factors in all cases.

Lycine pairs Heaven with Earth ☰ ☷ and with Mountain ☰ ☶ to give the hexagrams ䷊ , Peace, and ䷙ , The taming power of the great, corresponding to the codons AAA and AAG. The appropriate readings are:

Lycine: *Nos. 11 and 26.*

11. Peace.

The image is of heaven within earth, a time of peace and prosperity, when rulers have careful regard of those whom they lead, and those more lowly appreciate and honour their rulers. The good elements of society are in control and the evil elements are influenced by them and change for the better.

26. The taming power of the great.

The main motif here is that of 'holding firm'. This is expressed in three ways: Heaven within the Mountain gives the idea of holding together; Keeping still restraining the strong gives the idea of 'holding back'; and thirdly is the idea of holding in the sense of caring for and nourishing the worthy.

Common theme: These are good times, when strong but good rulers are in control. They exercise care over the weaker in society, and seek genuine progress for all.

Glutamic Acid pairs Heaven with both Thunder ☰ ☳ and with Fire ☰ ☲ so we should expect strong themes again. The hexagrams are ䷡,The power of the great & ䷍,Possession in great measure, corresponding to the codons GAA and GAG. The readings are:

Glutamic Acid: Nos. 34 and 14.

34. The power of the great.

This speaks of a time when powerful men are in control, but warns of the dangers inherent unless they adhere to the fundamental principles of righteousness and justice. Once again there is the danger of slipping into chaos, as we have seen happen so often in, for instance, the Middle East.

14. Possession in great measure.

This also is directed ostensibly at government, and like the reading above speaks of a time of peace and plenty because the ruler is modest, unassuming, but capable of holding all together.

 Common theme: The blessings of living in a well-governed country, where those in control are good men. In our own individual lives this corresponds to governing ourselves well, not giving in to base desires, but tending the higher parts of our nature.

We are left with the three stop hexagrams, corresponding to what are called the Ochre, Amber and Opal stops of mRNA, with codons respectively UAA, UAG and UGA. The corresponding hexagrams are ䷟, Duration (Marriage), ䷱, The Great bowl (sacred vessel) and ䷡, Great heaviness. The common trigram is ☴, Wood/wind, and indeed it appears also in the last, single hexagram ䷫, Encountering (Coming to meet) with its associated codon UGG, which produces Tryptophan. The Wood/Wind attribute of gentle penetration presumably will influence all four readings.

The stop hexagrams: Nos. 32, 50 and 28.

32. Duration (Marriage).

It is far from obvious that this should represent the beginnings of a command to stop, as it does in an mRNA reading. However, the Judgement reads:

Duration is continuity in change.
Duration succeeds through self-renewal.

This does in fact have the air of an ending, an ending that will enable a new beginning, and Wilhelm's expanded text reads 'Each end is reached by inhalation, contraction; an inward movement. It becomes a new beginning in exhalation, expansion: where the movement is directed outwards.' It goes on to give the examples of heavenly bodies waxing and waning, and of the seasons regular changing.

50. The great bowl (sacred vessel).

Likewise, at first sight this doesn't look like any sort of command to 'get ready to stop'. But again, the judgement speaks of the time as being the culmination of culture, the high point of a society's life. By the laws of change, things will now go downhill. The wood that feeds the fire in the image needs constantly to be renewed, and it is that end and new beginning that is signalled here.

28. Great heaviness.

The image here is of a ridgepole of a house which is thick and heavy in the middle, but thin and weak at the ends. The condition is extraordinary, and must end. Change must come, or all is lost.

Common theme: The readings posit increasingly critical end-points, where a new beginning is desperately needed. They are indeed appropriate to the Ochre, Amber and Opal codons that signify 'Stop' in mRNA.

Lastly, Tryptophan corresponds to reading 44:

Tryptophan : *44. Coming to meet.*

This represents a dangerous situation where the dark principle (yin), having been banished, suddenly returns (in the bottom line of the hexagram) and becomes ascendant. In ordinary life this refers to the situation where a person has managed to break a bad or dangerous habit, or a wrong affair, and thinks he can now afford to dally with the danger. This does in fact share some characteristics of the Stop hexagrams, extending the idea to that of making a permanent stop,

179

whereas the three above envisage a stop only to allow a fresh beginning.

This completes the survey of all 64 hexagrams, split into the groups corresponding to groups of codons which produce the same amino acid. Obviously it is a subjective judgement as to whether I have succeeded in demonstrating that the situations signified by the groups of codons are also genuinely in homogenous groups, but I offer the following extension to the great table in the hopes it may be acceptable. Here I have left out the codons and the amino acid names, inserting instead what I consider to be the appropriate group name for the situations described by the hexagrams in the group, and the hexagram numbers in the normal text.

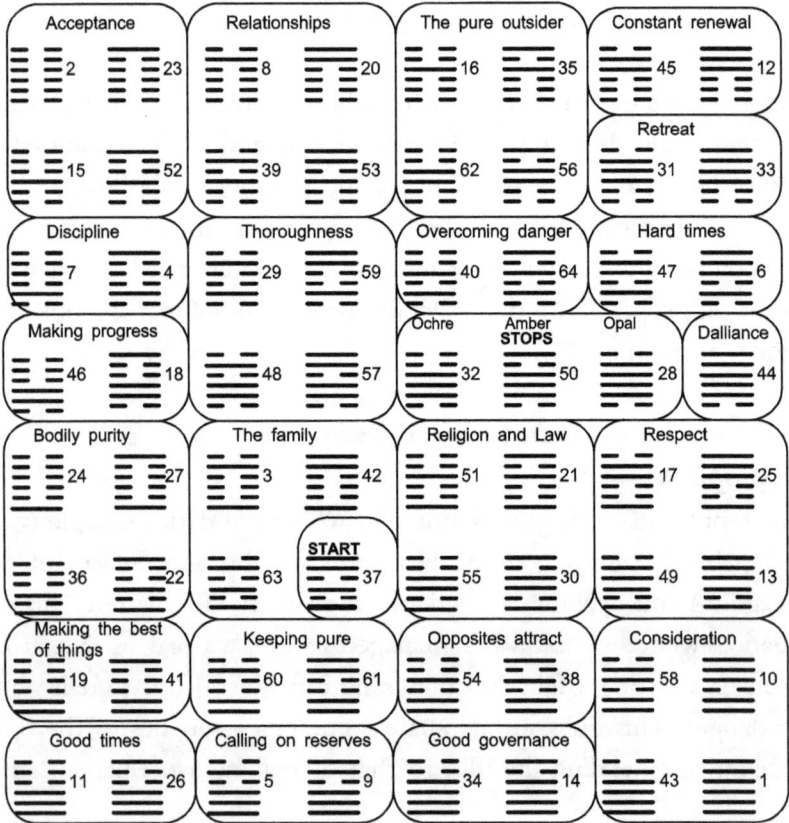

Acceptance — 2, 23, 15, 52

Relationships — 8, 20, 39, 53

The pure outsider — 16, 35, 62, 56

Constant renewal — 45, 12

Retreat — 31, 33

Discipline — 7, 4

Thoroughness — 29, 59

Overcoming danger — 40, 64

Hard times — 47, 6

Making progress — 46, 18, 48, 57

Ochre — 32

Amber STOPS — 50

Opal — 28

Dalliance — 44

Bodily purity — 24, 27

The family — 3, 42

Religion and Law — 51, 21

Respect — 17, 25

36, 22, 63, START 37, 55, 30, 49, 13

Making the best of things — 19, 41

Keeping pure — 60, 61

Opposites attract — 54, 38

Consideration — 58, 10

Good times — 11, 26

Calling on reserves — 5, 9

Good governance — 34, 14, 43, 1

Conclusion

A unified theory of being

If one were able to accept all the arguments put forward in this book it would lead to the conclusion that we human beings operate on a complementary basis in the three areas of our lives: the physical, the psychological, and what, for want of a better word, we might call the spiritual. That is to say, one fundamental pattern governs all three aspects of our lives, and it is the simplest 8 x 8 matrix of the counting numbers written in binary form, from 0 to 63.

As we have seen, this matrix groups all the 64 codons with which our DNA maintains our physical life in precisely the groupings worked out by bio-chemists from 1961onwards. We have also seen that the same matrix arranges all 64 hexagrams of the I Ching again in identical groups which can also be seen to apply to 22 common situations we are likely to find ourselves in. My thesis is, then, that just as ribosomes read long strips of mRNA in order to split it into codons which attract the 20 amino acids which maintain our physical body, so the ribosomes reading the mRNA in our limbic brains maintain the collective unconscious housed there, which we share with all humanity.

This collective unconscious can remain in our unconscious, without our being aware of its very existence, but it will nevertheless affect our personality, our reactions to situations, and our relationships. We become more rounded personalities if we are able to access these unknown knowns, bringing them into the realm of consciousness. This is where the I Ching has a role to play. It is by no means the only way of accessing our unconscious, but because it shares the same 8 x 8 matrix of the binary numbers with the codon map it has a direct access which is not apparent in more traditional approaches such as prayer, fasting and asceticism. I would claim it is, in fact, a form of prayer – a prayer which receives an answer if we will take the time to ponder the particular reading which is indicated by our question.

The reason this form of prayer is so direct is that the only God we can have any apprehension of is also to be found in this collective unconscious. This is not to confirm or deny God's existence: He/She/It may well be 'the First Cause', but we can know nothing about that aspect of the universe. All we can know is this 'God within' (Jung's phrase), which is the same God for all humanity, whatever the individual names given. And we cannot truly be atheists, even if we rationally believe there is no God, because the God involved in our collective unconscious is a shared human reality, whether we recognise it or not.

However, those who refuse to recognise this unconscious are the poorer for it, for our 'unknown knowns' are a critical part of our being human, and seeking them out is the most satisfying journey we can take. They tie us to all humankind, of whatever race, colour or creed, and they hold the answer to all of life's fundamental questions.

Bibliography

BOARDMAN, W.S. *The Pocket I Ching*. ISBN 0-14-019049-X

DODDS, E.R.. *The Greeks and the Irrational*. ISBN 978-0-520-24230-2

JUNG, CARL GUSTAV. *The Archetypes and the Collective Unconscious*. Translated by R.F.C. Hull. ISBN 978-0-415-05844-5.

JUNG, CARL GUSTAV. *Four Archetypes*. Translated by R.F.C. Hull. ISBN 978-0-691-15049-9.

JUNG, CARL GUSTAV. *Synchronicity – an acausal connecting principle*. Translated by R.F.C. Hull. ISBN 0 7100 7416 6.

JUNG, CARL GUSTAV. *Psychology and Religion*. ISBN 978-0-300-00137-2

JUNG, CARL GUSTAV & PAULI, WOLFGANG. *Atom and the Archetype – the Pauli/Jung letters*. Edited by C.A. Meier. ISBN 0-691-01207-5.

LEGGE, JAMES. *I Ching – Book of Changes (1996 ed.)*. ISBN 0-517-14990-7.

LIMAR, IGOR V. *C.G. Jung's synchronicity and quantum entanglement*, published in the journal 'NeuroQuantology' – (2011) Volume 9, Issue 2, pp 313-321

MILLER, ARTHUR I. *137 Jung, Pauli, and the pursuit of a scientific obsession*. ISBN 978-0-393-33864-5.

RADIN, DEAN. *Entangled Minds: extrasensory experiences in a quantum reality*. ISBN 978-1-4165-1677-4

SCHÖNBERGER, DR. MARTIN. *The I Ching and the Genetic Code.* Translated by D.Q. Stephenson. ISBN 0-943358-37-X.

SPECTOR, TIM. *Identically Different – why you can change your genes.* ISBN: 978-1-7802-2090-1.

WALTER, KATYA. *Tao of Chaos.* ISBN 1-85230-806-0

WILHELM, RICHARD. *I Ching or Book of Changes.* Translated by Cary F. Baynes. ISBN 978-0-140-19207-0.

IAN HALL

Ian Hall has been, variously, a Maths teacher, a builder, a Lakeland fell farmer, a campsite operator and the owner of several self-catering properties in the Lake District (most of these occupations shared with Jennifer, his wife).

He also trained with the Carlisle Diocesan Training Institute to become a Church of England Non-Stipendiary Minister, assisting a succession of vicars in the Eskdale group of parishes.

Since retirement he and Jennifer have lived near Keswick, close to the school where they first met as young teenagers.

He is the author 'Fisherground – Living the Dream', a memoir of their quarter-century spent fell-farming in Eskdale valley in partnership with their friends Geoff and Anne-Marie Wake.

www.ingramcontent.com/pod-product-compliance
Lightning Source LLC
LaVergne TN
LVHW051303080426
835509LV00020B/3139